Proceedings of the
5th Rocky Mountain Region
Disaster Mental Health Conference

Edited by George W. Doherty, MS, LPC

ISBN-13 978-1-932690-37-8
ISBN-10 1-932690-37-9

ROCKY MOUNTAIN REGION DISASTER MENTAL HEALTH INSTITUTE
PO BOX 786
LARAMIE, WY 82073-0786

http://www.rmrinstitute.org/rocky.html
email: rockymountain@mail2emergency.com
Phone: 307-399-4818

The Rocky Mountain Region Disaster Mental Health Institute is a 501(c)3 Non-profit Organization.

Table of Contents

Foreword

Since 1998, the Rocky Mountain Region Disaster Mental Health Institute has pursued the mission of promoting the development and application of practice, research and training in disaster mental health, critical incident stress management, traumatology and other emergency response interventions and the promotion of community awareness, resilience and recovery. This includes hazards vulnerability, mitigation research, strategic planning, and training for first responders, mental health professionals, chaplains and related personnel in all settings. The Institute's motto is: "Learning from the past and planning for the future."

One of the Institute's purposes includes providing a forum for presentation of research results, practice activities, field experiences and other opportunities for networking. The Fifth Annual Rocky Mountain Region Disaster Mental Health Conference was an opportunity for first responders and mental health professionals to present and discuss information about their experiences in the field and to share this with peers. An additional objective for this conference was to give presenters and delegates the opportunity to briefly pull away from their response modes and to decompress in a pleasant environment with peers who share their understanding of how these stressful events and responses affect not just victims, but also responders and mental health professionals.

The theme of the conference was "TAKING CHARGE IN TROUBLED TIMES: Response, Resilience, Recovery and Follow-up." Presenters addressed various aspects of this topic and further discussed these with delegates in a number of daily roundtable discussions. After hours, delegates were able to take part in a number of planned and ad-hoc activities.

Again, the conference had two goals: one to learn from research, field experiences and networking; and second, to provide a safe, fun, relaxing time to enjoy away from regular responder activities. In both of these, the conference was a success. This book presents major papers and information about the presentations and activities. It is hoped that this volume will allow further dissemination of these presentations to others in the first responder and disaster mental health communities and provide a useful addition to these very important fields. This book is dedicated to all those first responders (fire, law enforcement, EMTs, disaster mental health professionals, chaplains and others) who are always there for victims of disasters and critical incidents and who help each other in dealing with the stresses of such response. Without these dedicated people, we all would be less resilient

—George W. Doherty, President
Rocky Mountain Region
Disaster Mental Health Institute

Acknowledgements

In preparing for and carrying out a conference such as this, it takes the work and cooperation of many individuals. Thanks are due to Carol Chapin, Director of Convention Sales for the Casper Area Convention and Visitors Bureau and her very able staff. All delegates were treated to a reception buffet dinner at the Casper Events Center, sponsored by the Visitors Bureau. Additional thanks are extended to: the Mayor of Casper, The Honorable Renee R. Burgess for welcoming the conference delegates; to Bruce Berst, Company I, who presented the story of the Platte Bridge Station and Red Butte Battle (both including information about Caspar Collins for whom the city of Casper is named); Carol Chapin who presented the story of the City of Casper—its transformation from cattle town to the Oil Capital of the Rockies; the volunteer workers from the Visitors Bureau who assisted at the reception and those who helped work registration at the conference; Renee Penton-Jones, General Manager and LeAnn Miller, Director of Catering and their staffs at the Casper Holiday Inn on the River for their professional assistance in the logistics of making the onsite activities of the conference a success.

Others that contributed to the success of the conference included David Smith, Gary Hulit, Randy Hanson, Stewart Anderson, Theresa Simpson, Merit Thomas and others who helped spread the word about the conference among their colleagues. Among those to whom we are further indebted are the Casper Petroleum Club and their able staff for opening their dining facility for our Conference Delegate Dinner on the Friday evening of the conference. Finally, thanks to Jude Carino, Center Director, National Historic Trails Interpretive Center for making available discounted admissions passes to the Center for conference attendees. Delegates who took advantage of this experienced the unique opportunity of learning about the history of the early pioneers traveling west and the hardships they encountered from interpretive talks, exhibits and interactive activities.

Cheyenne, WY

John Durkin
Ely, Cambridgeshire
United Kingdom

Patricia Justice
Docklands Counseling &
Psychotherapy Services
London, England

Peak Wellness Center

Daniel R. Bogart, MA,LPC
Evanston, WY

Shawna Kautzman
Laramie, WY

Laramie, WY

Rev Bob Rudichar
Campbell County
    Memorial Hospital
Gillette, WY

Taking Charge In Troubled Times:
Response, Resilience, Recovery and Follow-up

George W. Doherty, MS, LPC
President, Rocky Mountain Region Disaster Mental Health Institute

Abstract

Recent years have seen an extraordinary number of major disasters, critical incidents and other events that have had major impacts on our world. The 2004 tsunami, hurricanes Rita and Katrina, and the wars in Iraq and Afghanistan affect millions of lives daily. Potential events such as Avian Flu pandemic, global warming and the increasing threats of spreading unrest in the Middle East are concerns that weigh heavily on all. Resilience, recovery from crises and how to prepare communities, learn from past experience, and strategically plan for future events are all activities that involve the education, training and time of first responders and mental health professionals. This paper briefly presents an overview of resilience assessment and planning and then an overview of the major papers presented at the Fifth Annual Rocky Mountain Region Disaster Mental Health Conference held in Casper, Wyoming November 8-11, 2007.

In recent years, the world has been exposed to many events and incidents that were and continue to be traumatic in their effects on all involved whether primary responders and/or as secondary ones or even vicariously. Victims of these events continue to be affected as well. The year 2005 began with a tsunami in south Asia. It was a year with a record number of Atlantic hurricanes—at least three of which wreaked havoc on major population centers. The war in the Middle East continued. Returning veterans and their families are facing new challenges upon re-entry into their home communities. The movement of "Bird Flu" around the world and its potential for a possible pandemic has prompted health officials to seek preparation with communities for how to deal with such an event should the virus mutate so that human-to-human transmission occurs. How to involve mental health professionals is important. The topic of global warming still presents major concerns. Cultural sensitivity is an additional factor of continuing concern in planning how best to respond to disasters and critical incidents locally, nationally and internationally.

Appropriate ethical responses by disaster mental health professionals is an emerging topic of concern. What are the traumatic effects of hurricanes Rita and Katrina one year later—among responders, victims and especially among those who remain in other parts of the country? How does resilience affect recovery from disasters and critical incidents. What are the continuing effects on children? How do local communities identify and prepare for hazards in their communities? What role does mental health prepare for and play with Red Cross, CISM, first responders, victims, Homeland Security, Military, and emergency management? These questions and others were ones addressed and discussed at the Fifth Annual Rocky Mountain Region Disaster Mental Health Conference held in Casper, Wyoming November 8-11, 2006.

Resilience: Assessment and Planning

There are a number of factors which support individuals, families and communities which help to minimize the consequences of disasters in terms of supporting preparedness activities as well as supporting sustaining recovery activities. Some of them are the reverse of vulnerability such as access and adequate resources. Identifying and assessing those positive factors possessed or shared by individuals, families, groups, communities and agencies which support resilience gives emergency planners and managers the opportunity to further develop resilience to increase the "disaster resistance" of the population.

Communities and agencies may be vulnerable to loss and damage from emergencies or disasters. A similar process of assessing elements of vulnerability and resilience and evaluating capability can be undertaken for communities and agencies as is undertaken for assessing the vulnerability and resilience of individuals, families, households, and groups. It is important to emphasize in the vulnerability assessment that vulnerabilities and needs may change over time. Needs may be significantly less in terms of numbers of people and the urgency of the need after a few hours than after days or weeks. For example, the loss of a water supply may be trivial for an hour or two, but for much longer than that it has the potential to affect the whole population in a critical way. Time of year may also be an important factor in assessing vulnerability and, hence, potential. Loss of heating in summer is less significant than it is in winter. Likewise, loss of refrigeration in winter may be less critical than in summer.

A resilience and vulnerability profile is an integral element of effective planning in the management of consequences to a community in an emergency or disaster. Resilience can be taken to be the capacity of a group or organization to withstand loss or damage or to recover from the impact of an emergency or disaster. Vulnerability is a broad measure of the susceptibility to suffer loss or damage. The higher the resilience, the less likely damage may be, and the faster and more effective recovery is likely to be. Conversely, the higher vulnerability is, the more exposed to loss and damage is the household, community or organization.

Resilience and vulnerability assessment is a process that is a necessary component of effective emergency management planning. However, it is unlikely that any assessment, or community audit, will capture every potential need or identify every person who, in some circumstance, may be exposed to a risk or to the possibility of some loss. This suggests that following an emergency or disaster it will be necessary to scan the affected area, through information campaigns, outreach programs, letterbox drops, and other methods, to identify people who require assistance.

Any resilience and vulnerability analysis needs to be conducted with sensitivity and proper regard for people's privacy. This includes their right not to provide information. Additionally, due regard must be paid to the legal and other requirements of maintaining appropriate standards of confidentiality when dealing with information from the public. This information can be used as guidelines to assist planning by community members, emergency managers, etc. engaged in emergency prevention or response or recovery activities. It can be used by emergency managers from any level of community or organizational level as well.

Conducting a resilience and vulnerability analysis is not an end in itself. The purpose behind such activity is to highlight issues, needs and concerns and to work to effect a change—to improve resilience and/or to reduce vulnerability.

Once the vulnerability assessment has been undertaken, the results will identify special needs which can be directly addressed as part of the local emergency management process. The results of the assessment should directly inform the process of planning, prevention and preparedness and may be made available to individuals, groups, communities and agencies to assist them with their local activity.

Significance

Mental Health Services before, during and following disasters, critical incidents, crises, and terrorist activities are becoming an integral part of disaster and critical incident preparedness, mitigation, response, and follow-up. Disaster Mental Health Services is a relatively new field which has expanded significantly within the past ten years. Critical Incident Stress Management and related interventions have been around since the early 1980s and, in one form or another since WW II. In order to continue to grow and meet identified needs, both require continued development as well as focused research, training and ongoing strategic planning. Research will help identify how Mental Health Services can best be utilized as well as how relevant changes need to be made in practice. Networking and sharing experiences can also help develop resources. Ongoing training and updates from the field help mental health professionals and first responders to remain on the same page when responding. Strategic planning can help prepare responders and mental health professionals for their respective roles in a real event.

The long-term goal includes training emergency Disaster Mental Health teams and CISM teams to conduct interventions for corporations, states, municipalities and rural communities in the Rocky Mountain region and other parts of the country and to evaluate their effectiveness in reducing the effects of trauma on first responders and others as well as affected communities and organizations.

Fifth Annual Rocky Mountain Region Disaster Mental Health Conference Papers

In order to help promote dissemination of relevant information presented at the Fifth Annual Rocky Mountain Region Disaster Mental Health Conference, presenters were asked to submit papers for publication. Those who responded to this call have their papers included in this volume. Additional presentations are summarized in an additional article included herein.

In a thoughtful and discussion-provoking paper, Alan Hensley analyzes why good people go bad from a psychosocial viewpoint of events that occurred at Abu Ghraib. This was a hastily created detention facility used to contain individuals who jeopardized potential success in Iraq. Inmates represented a perceived threat to a greatly outnumbered guard force. Few, if any spoke English. A large contingent of CIA and contract former military counter-intelligence officers were assigned and were provided a wide degree of latitude in how they operated. Hensley contends that the Department of Defense neglected to recognize such variables and concerns as Maslow's hierarchy of needs, group schema theory, the effects of fear and sleep deprivation, or take advantage of information resulting from Zimbardo's (2004) Stanford Prison Experiment of the 1970's. He suggests that looking at these factors would have been helpful in predicting the outcome of Abu Ghraib in forewarning about key thinking errors and in predicting the potential for posttraumatic stress among the guards. Hensley offers practical solutions that may have helped prevent the embarrassment of Abu Ghraib and other highly visible alleged atrocities in

Operation Enduring Freedom and Operation Iraqi Freedom (OEF/OIF). He further argues that we are creating a generation that will create an unprecedented strain on the nation's medical and mental healthcare system which is likely to become multi-generational. Information in Hensley's paper can be generalized in some respects to responses in other environments such as those seen in Hurricane Katrina.

In the Role of Culture and Cultural Sensitivity in Disaster Response, Hensley also reports on and responds to the contents of one of the conference roundtable discussions. New Orleans and the gulf region experienced the most intense natural disaster in recent United States history. The city of Philadelphia offered to provide care, shelter, and treatment for gulf families in Philadelphia. WES Corporation, Pennsylvania's largest African American managed behavioral health organization, was asked to provide emergency assessment, triage, and treatment. In their paper, Glass and Graves highlight the process of developing effective and culturally competent services for victims of a natural disaster in a short time frame in an ethical manner. They discuss services, including: understanding the clinician's ethical challenges in natural disasters; creating culturally competent care and privacy in an emergency situation; articulating the unique aspects of engaging families of varying ethnic backgrounds in a temporary setting; and balancing your existing work with new demands.

What is it like living in a state of perpetual war and terror? Tragedy put in its appearance at Mike's Place after midnight on a Wednesday in April 2003. Mike's Place is a rock and roll bar next to the American Embassy in Tel Aviv, Israel. On April 23, 2003, two well-dressed young men with British passports approached. Avi Tabib was the security guard who sensed something unusual about these customers and confronted them at the curb. The explosion that followed killed four, including the terrorist, and wounded over fifty. Avi survived, but experienced a long and painful recovery. Based on interviews with Avi and other survivors, Curtis and Faudem present details about his resiliency and the fortitude of coworkers who reopened Mike's Place on Israel's Independence Day one week after the attack. As part of their presentation, a documentary film *Blues By The Beach*, made by Faudem and his associates, showed footage. of the suicide bomber as he exploded himself on Jam Nite. The film also showed the effects of terror, the aftermath and moving on. In their paper, Curtis and Faudem discuss these events.

John Durkin discusses how the National Health Service in the United Kingdom follows guidelines on the treatment of Posttraumatic Stress Disorder (PTSD) that demand cognitive behavior therapy (CBT), Eye Movement Desensitization and Reprocessing (EMDR) and drug therapies. He further discusses concerns that are emerging that this "medical model" viewpoint of stress may be restraining innovation and limiting progress. Durkin suggests that viewing stress in a person-centered way may offer a practical, flexible and potentially superior alternative to the medical model. Using Traumatic Incident Reduction (TIR) as an example of a person-centered approach, he challenges the relevance of formal diagnosis and treatment to the resolution of distress.

Hensley also presents a case study about a woman identified as suffering from Dissociative Identity Disorder (DID). He discusses the use of Traumatic Incident Reduction (TIR) as an approach to this intriguing and complicated case.

In October 2005, the United States Department of Health and Human Services published a warning of a new influenza pandemic. It proposed a scenario in which 8.5 million Americans would be hospitalized and 1.9 million would die. In the event of such a catastrophe or of a bio-logical/chemical terrorism attack, over-extended local medical facilities would be confronted by a crush of non-exposed citizens while trying to deal with those who have been infected. In his paper, Thom Curtis, Ph.D. proposes a role for disaster mental health workers in assisting the medical community to triage and separate the sick from those merely worried.

In 2005, Patricia Justice visited as a Volunteer the worst hit area of Thailand after the 2004 tsunami. She has returned four times to the same area to follow up on the progress in Khoa Lak where over 6,000 lives were lost. Many of the bodies have still not been identified and lie in re-frigerated trucks in the same area. Survivors still do not know whether their loved ones bodies will ever be returned to them or are lost forever. In 2006, Justice also did follow-up work in Sri Lanka. In her paper, she discusses the impact on those people who work or worked with the survivors. She also points out that little is known about the impacts on the workers. Justice her-self was involved in a near fatal car crash in April 2006 and in her paper she discusses how the survivors of the tsunami "cared for me". Topics she addresses include: How long can those di-rectly involved keep going? What effect does it have on them and their families? What preparation do they need for future events? Can we do anything to prevent secondary trauma-tization for workers? In 1996, Justice was involved as a trauma therapist following the Docklands Bomb (ex IRA) in London, England. At the time, she also researched the experience of counselors and Critical Incident Debriefing from this event. In her paper, she discusses some of her findings. She also presents her own experiences of working in both Thailand and Sri Lanka following the tsunami on December 24th, 2004. She concludes with a plea for recogni-tion that care for caregivers is an important area of concern for responders to consider in preparation for future events.

The fields of critical incident response, crisis intervention, and disaster mental health are in constant flux and evolve with every major disaster. Every week the headlines reflect terrorism, natural disasters, and fears of pandemics. New information comes out regularly. This makes it necessary to keep those who must meet these challenges abreast of important changes as they occur. Ongoing training and updates based on changes in the field and evidence-informed feedback from field experience and research is crucial to maintaining appropriate and high lev-els of training among instructors, responders and mental health professionals. The International Critical Incident Stress Foundation (ICISF), in partnership with Weber State Uni-versity has undertaken an on-line learning initiative intended to help broaden the availability of updated training material to those involved in the crisis and disaster mental health fields. In his paper, Richard Conroy discusses the grant funding Weber State University received to ex-plore the expansion of critical incident stress management training in the western United States, One of the grant objectives is to make training information available to students in new and innovative ways. The pilot course developed for online access is titled *The Changing Face of Crisis and Disaster Mental Health Intervention*. The course is designed to provide an ongoing up-date in the fields of critical incident response, crisis intervention, and disaster mental health. Conroy emphasizes that updates provide access to the latest trends, theories, and practices.

Major factors affecting families with military members include war-zone military service, family separation, and readjustment back into the community by service members. Posttrau-matic stress (including PTSD) and psychosocial malfunctioning are among problems encountered. Strengths that contribute to resiliency by all family members include religious values, a positive outlook on life events, family support and various forms of psycho-social interventions (Apellaniz, 1999). Debbie Russell presents information about Family Assistance Centers (FAC's) in Wyoming and their responses in support of all DOD deployed families, all services, and all components. The FACs are critical links for Service Members, families, commands and the community. They are strategically placed within the state to overcome the large geographic distances that frequently separate families from centralized, installation-based services. The FACs are the primary entry point for assistance for all Service Members regardless of Service Component. They provide information, referral, and outreach to Service Members and families during the deployment process—preparation (pre-deployment), sustainment (actual deployment), and reunion (reintegration). Such services are vital to the welfare of families during deployments. They also provide critical assistance to demobilizing Service Members and promote the long-term health and welfare of the military family. FACs also provide information and services for retirees and Veterans. Russell's contribution provides mental health professionals and first responders with information and resources available to increase awareness of how to effectively respond to and assist with families of deployed Service Members in rural areas such as Wyoming.

Summary

The presenters, presentations and delegates at this conference represented the various areas and issues that the fields of disaster mental health, trauma, and critical incident response are facing in our continually changing world. With the challenges of terrorism, natural and man-made disasters, global warming, hazardous material events, air, auto, housefire disasters, wildfires, floods and other critical incidents seeming to be more pervasive in recent years, it is incumbent upon responders, mental health professionals and emergency managers to continually update and increase their education, training and planning to be able to effectively respond to future events. Families of deployed military personnel and their returning relatives and friends will need all of us to be there for them now and when they return home. It is critical that we as responders and mental health professionals network with and assist where we can with military and veteran groups and others in order to accomplish the goals in which we each believe.

About the Author

George W. Doherty has held positions as counselor/therapist, Masters Level psychologist, consultant, educator, and disaster mental health specialist and is a former U.S. Air Force Officer, Connally Navigator, USAF. Currently, he serves as President of O`Dochartaigh Associates, a position he has held since 1985. He is also President and CEO of the Rocky Mountain Region Disaster Mental Health Institute. He has served as a Masters Psychologist for Rural Clinics Community Counseling Center (State of Nevada) in Ely, NV, an Adjunct Instructor the University of Wyoming, an Adjunct Instructor for Northern Nevada Community College, currently an Adjunct Faculty member of Kennedy-Western University. He is a Certified Instructor, International Critical Incident Stress Foundation (ICISF), Certified WY POST Instructor. Editorial Board, *PsycCRITIQUES,* Level II Member of International Critical Incident Stress Foundation and. Member, Traumatic Incident Reduction Association (TIRA), Associate Member of the American Psychological Association, Life Member of the Air Force Association, Life Member of the Penn State Alumni Association. Member American Counseling Association, Life Member of the Military Officers Association of America and serves as an Alumni Admissions Volunteer with The Pennsylvania State University. He has served in the Civil Air Patrol (an Air Force Auxiliary) as a Squadron Commander, Deputy Wing Commander, Air Operations Officer and Master Observer,

REFERENCES

Apellaniz, Ilia Maria (April 1999). Coping with war enforced separation: A pilot study on the account of wives of Puerto Rican civilian soldiers. *Dissertation Abstracts International: Section B: The Sciences & Engineering,* Vol 59(10-B), pp. 5567.

Zimbardo, P. (2004). *Stanford prison experiment: A simulation study of the psychology of imprisonment conducted at Stanford University.* Retrieved on September 27, 2005 from http://www.prisonexp.org/

Why Good People Go Bad:
A Case Study of the Abu Ghraib Prison Abuse Courts-Martial
Alan L. Hensley, PhD Candidate, BCETS, FAAETS

Abstract

Problems cannot be solved at the same level of awareness that created them. More than three years have elapsed since the revelation of the abuses at the Abu Ghraib Prison. Careers have been ruined and lives inextricably altered. Ten court-martials have occurred, with another soon approaching. However, the endemic factors that led to the abuses have yet to be addressed. This article addresses the events in context of well-grounded psychological, sociological, and criminological theory and research.

Introduction

More than three years have elapsed since Military Police Sergeant Joseph Darby first alerted the U.S. Criminal Justice Command to alleged prisoner abuse at Abu Ghraib Prison complex. To support his allegation, Darby provided a compact disc of images of naked prisoners, being forced into homosexual activity and other degrading acts as American military men and women looked on. The revelations sparked one of the most intense investigations undertaken in Operation Iraqi Freedom.

In April 2004, the television program, *60 Minutes* broke the story of the alleged abuse of prisoners with graphic pictures to the world. The images sparked international outrage. To quell the furor, it became apparent that the military hierarchy must demonstrate disapproval of the behavior of the participating members of the 372nd Military Police Battalion.

In July 2003, General Sanchez, Commanding Officer of the United Central Command, relieved Brigadier General Janis Karpenski of command of the facility, replacing her with Major General Geoffrey Miller, former Commander of the controversial Guantanamo Bay Detention Facility in Cuba.

Eleven other persons formerly assigned to Abu Ghraib have since been subjected to court martial. Each defendant has been found guilty of violation of the Uniform Code of Military Justice (UCMJ) and sentenced accordingly. To the population not indoctrinated in the effects and comorbidity associated with complex traumatic stress, the problem has been resolved. However, the author suggests that the chosen solution has merely produced a scab on an insidious wound.

It is widely recognized that problems cannot be solved at the same level of awareness that created them. To understand and address the causal factors, one must first study the etiology that defines the environment that produced the problematic behavior.

The Situation

As Coalition Forces assumed control of Iraq, the question remained of what to do with the thousands of prisoners taken into custody. Perceived as the most viable immediate solution was the notorious Abu Ghraib Prison, located twenty miles west of Baghdad. During the

Ba'athist regime of Saddam Hussein, the Abu Ghraib Prison had a reputation as a place of torture and execution of thousands of political prisoners. However, during the collapse of the Hussein Regime, the facility was stripped of any artifact that could be removed; including doors, windows, toilets, showers, and even large sections of brick. Hurriedly, the Coalition had the cells cleaned and repaired. Toilets, showers, and a new medical facility were added.

Oddly, Brigadier General Janis Karpinski, a Reserve Intelligence Officer, without any training in correctional facility operation, was placed in charge of all of the military prisons in Iraq. In June of 2003, Karpenski found herself in charge of three large prisons, eight battalions, and 3,400 Army Reservists. Most of those persons she commanded, like herself, had no training or experience in correctional operations. Despite the obvious shortcomings, the prison population, which at times reportedly exceeded as many as 50,000 detainees, soon included high-value leaders of the insurgency against the coalition forces, others suspected of crimes against the coalition, as well as common criminals. Taguba noted in ex-post-facto testimony that the facility was filled beyond capacity and the guards were greatly outnumbered and short of resources. In addition to repeatedly requesting additional personnel, supplies, and other assistance, Karpinski had repeated requested to release the prisoners deemed not to present a threat to Coalition Forces; her request were repeatedly ignored or denied. Few, if any of the detainees spoke English, nor did the Coalition guards speak Arabic. During Karpinski's seven-month Command, there were at least a dozen officially reported incidents involving escapes, attempted escapes, and other serious security issues. Some of the incidents had resulted in killing or injuring of detainees as well as MPs. Thus, the stage was set for maximum apprehension and fear.

Additionally, the Islamic male detainees experienced an unprecedented heinous situation—female guards. Such a situation is considered unacceptable in the Arab world—a fact well known to the military planners. Thus, the detainees were further infuriated at the lack of sociocultural understanding and treatment.

The abuse subsequently revealed to the world and described in graphic detail in the ten Courts-martial to date, suggests that the abuse was a routine occurrence; so common, in fact, that the soldiers felt little need to hide it. Much of the physical abuse described in the Courts-martial proceedings appear to have been the product of Staff Sergeant Frederick and Corporal Graner, with the others participating in lesser dehumanizing acts. During the court martial of Frederick, the Defense Council argued that Frederick often noted in letters and e-mails to family members that CIA Officers and contract linguists and interrogation specialists were the dominant forces inside the prisons directing the operations. In one such letter, Frederick expressed concern of practices such as leaving a prisoner in an isolation cell with little or no clothes, no toilet or running water, and no ventilation for several days.

The occurrences and emotions described by Frederick and others, without reprieve, leave little question of the effects of traumatic stress. However, in order to pacify the senses of those fortunate enough not to find themselves in such an involuntary predicament, these soldiers were subjected to additional traumatic stress, public and private humiliation, and a feeling of loss of control by subjecting them to criminal proceedings. However, Taguba recommended that the persons ultimately responsible for the environment, Colonel Thomas Pappas, commander of one of the military intelligence brigades was reprimanded and received non-judicial punishment; Colonel Stephen Jordan, former director of the Joint Interrogation and Briefing

Center, was relieved of command and reprimanded; and the civilian contractor, Stephen Stephanowicz, be fired from his Army job, reprimanded and denied a security clearance for ordering or allowing military policemen, who were not appropriately trained, to participate in military interrogation and lying to authorities. The difference between these punishments and those individuals subjected to Courts-martial—no Federal conviction. However, Taguba noted that he suspected these individuals were either directly or indirectly responsible for the conditions that led to the abuse. No criminal proceedings were suggested against Karpinski.

The Theories - A view from the primal level

Hensley (2004) suggested to the Area Defense Council involved in several of the Courts Martial proceedings that the abuses occurring at Abu Ghraib were largely predictable based upon well-established psychological and sociological theories and studies, including the Stanford Prison Experiment Model (Haney, Banks, & Zimbardo, 1973).

During the Court Martial of Jamal Davis, Major David DiNenna, Operations Officer of the 11th Military Police Brigade, stationed at Abu Ghraib from July 2003 to February 2004, described the conditions as "deplorable." Army Sgt. Kenneth Davis described Abu Ghraib as "[h]ell on earth... We were trying to help people and they're trying to kill us." More insightful is the statement by Davis, "I don't know what I was thinking. I shouldn't have done that. I am deeply sorry." Davis contended that the environment and atmosphere at Abu Ghraib contributed to his actions.

Dr. Philip Zimbardo, professor emeritus at Stanford University and expert witness at the Courts martial proceedings argued that the conditions at Abu Ghraib were the perfect medium in which the culture of guard violence could emerge and flourish. Dr. Ervin Staub, professor of Psychology, University of Massachusetts at Amherst also an expert witness in the courts martial proceedings, concurred in his opinion that the lawlessness and horrendous conditions at Abu Ghraib established the conditions necessary for prisoner abuse by soldiers as the atmosphere deteriorated sociologically and psychologically.

Individual Adaptation

Much of the human perception, cognition, and ultimately behavior is derived from the schema theory. Schemata refer to prototypical abstractions of complex concepts that are gradually developed from the cohesion of abstract facts and experience encountered during the socialization process. Over time, schemata evolve from discrete beliefs into more elaborately organized schemata, composed of many interrelated beliefs. Right or wrong, schemata then provide a framework of how we perceive, assess, understand, and react to incoming data without having to all associated objects and interrelationships each time a similar situation is encountered.

In abstraction, the influence of faulty schemata might be seen in a series of studies conducted by Dodge (1980) and his colleagues in whom the researchers found aggressive boys are more predisposed than their nonaggressive peers to interpret peers' intentions as hostile in an ambiguous situation. This phenomenon, commonly referred to as *hostile attribution bias*, was found to be more when children act quickly and unthinkingly to an ambiguous social situation (Dodge & Newman, 1981). Dodge, Petit, McClaskey, and Brown (1986), likewise, found aggressive children have specific deficits in the way that they process social information and cues in their environment, and in the way that they evaluate and react to these situations (See also Coie, Underwood, and Lochman, 1991). Most researchers investigating the information processing skills of aggressive children argue such children invoke schemata to process social cues and information. For example, Dodge and Tomlin (1987) opine aggressive children are more prone than nonaggressive peers are to base interpretations on schemata and experiences rather than actual social cues. A social exchange model constructed by Crick and Dodge (1994) found that frequent anger reactions of aggressive children to social interactions directly related to the activation of the individual's central database and schemata, which store social knowledge, rules, coping strategies, and memory. Unfortunately, researchers have also found that schemata are relatively durable and resistant to fundamental change after achieving a level of completeness with many linkages among their elements.

The author, therefore, opines that, while schemata perhaps serve the beneficial function of precluding the necessity to relearn the objects and internetworking of factors in a given situation, they can also cause a detriment to the individual and society in that they can diminish perception, objectivity, rational thought, and encourage bias and stereotyping; the embodiment being Abu Ghraib.

The Mental Model

Mental models, as executive agents, extend beyond schema theory to include perceptions of task demands and task performances. Once recalled, the mental model helps identify which information is most important for the task, what can be ignored or discarded, and how to interpret that information, which in the end influences our reaction or behavior. The author opines that a mental model is not required to be resident in the conscious mind to influence cognition and behavior. In many instances, recall may be subconscious and may be applied to a situation without being aware of it.

The author, then, argues that implicit knowledge comprising our schemata, in addition to providing a valuable timesaving function of providing a methodology for newly encountered phenomena, also provides a *mental filtering* function, constraining what can enter the cognitive system as new data to prevent *sensorial overload* or *informational inundation* of our cognitive capabilities. Despite the sociocultural similarities then, each person possesses an individualized conceptualization of reality; individually defining the importance of a particular object or behavior.

Perhaps the most salient aspect of the mental model and schema theories is the belief that the human mind strives for *consonance;* that is, people strive for cognitive consistency (consonance) in their own attitudes, beliefs, and personal values (Festinger, 1957).

Theory of Reasoned Action

The Theory of Reasoned Action (TRA) suggests people intend to behave in a manner that allows them to achieve favorable outcomes and meet the expectation of others (Ajzen & Fishbein, 1980). In TRA, behavioral intention is: 1) the product of the person's attitude toward the behavior, which includes behavioral beliefs concerning the potential outcomes of the behavior and positive or negative evaluation of the possible outcomes, and; 2) subjective norms, which include the perception of the sociocultural pressure to perform the behavior. Relying on the results of numerous studies, researchers argue that an individual's attitudes toward a behavior and subjective norms are, in fact, sufficient to determine behavioral intention (Bowman, & Fishbein, 1978; Goldenhar, & Connell, 1992; Jones).

Cognitive Dissonance

Cognitive dissonance, however, is "the state of psychological tension occurring when a choice has to be made between two equally attractive or equally unpleasant alternatives" (Hutchinson Encyclopedia, 2003). Consequently, that which does not favorably coincide with our perception of reality creates *cognitive dissonance*, which in turn, can result in a myriad of undesirable maladies, such as panic, fear, stress, depression, dependent upon our schematic experience. Festinger (1957) suggests dissonance occurs when a person's knowledge of their morals, values, feelings, desires, behavior, or knowledge of the world are inconsistent. Three conditions must exist for dissonance to occur; the decision needs to be important, irrevocable, and voluntary (Cummings & Venkatesan, 1976; Oliver, 1997).

Thus, cognitive dissonance forms when a decision is made, but cognition and opinion directs us in a different direction. The effects of dissonance usually remain after the decision has been made, motivating the individual to return to a state of equilibrium or consonance. The natural human tendency is to resolve the dissonance, or dismiss it as irrelevant or irrational.

What happens when one is not able to reconcile the dissonance created by the traumatic events experienced in their current environment with their mental model? For many, the carnage seen in Iraq and Afghanistan is unprecedented. A survey of 193,132 Department of Defense post-deployment assessments from January through August 2005, found 47% of the respondents had seen someone killed, wounded, or had seen a dead body. Fourteen percent experienced an event that left them easily startled. Six percent asked for help for stress, emotional, or substance abuse problems. Two percent expressed feelings of hurting someone or losing control and. One percent expressed feelings that they would be better off dead or have contemplated hurting themselves. More than 250 expressed that they have had such feelings "a lot."

In a larger sample returning from Iraq during the period of April 2003 through August 2005, a staggering 45% of over 538, 232 respondents reported feeling that they were in "great danger" of being killed during their deployment. Nineteen percent found little interest or pleasure in "doing things." Fourteen percent expressed feelings of depression and hopelessness. Nine percent suffered from nightmares or thoughts of undesirable experiences. In addition, three percent worried about domestic disputes (Zoroya, 2005).

These statistics are all indicators of post-traumatic stress disorder (PTSD) that should be of serious concern to American society (APA, 2000). PTSD occurs when an individual has been exposed to an overwhelming stressor (such as combat trauma, sexual/or physical assault, a terrorist attack, or a natural disaster) involving actual or threatened death or injury, or a threat to the physical integrity of him/herself or others (APA, 2000). During such exposure, the victim experiences an intense emotional response such as helplessness, loss of control, horror, or fear (Friedman, 2005; Van der Kolk, McFarlane, & Weisaeth, 1996; Najavits, L.M., 2002). Unquestionably, the untrained guards at Abu Ghraib Prison experienced these feelings.

While many who are exposed to the carnage of a combat environment will not develop PTSD, and many of those who do will quickly recover, others will develop PTSD and/or comorbid disorders. In fact, as many as one-quarter of the military men and women returning from Operation Iraqi Freedom (OIF) and Operation Enduring Freedom (OEF) suffer from PTSD (Engel, 2005). However, psychologists cannot point to a single individual with certainty to suggest they will, or will not, develop PTSD.

Frequently, the harmful effects of traumatic stress go unnoticed. Possible reasons range from the military macho image to lack of knowledge of the co-morbid presentation of physical, mental, emotional, and behavioral disorders, such as disorders, especially depression, other anxiety disorders, and alcohol/substance abuse (Friedman, 2005; Najavits, 2002). This fact is unfortunate in that PTSD prevention is seen as being predicated upon early intervention (van der Kolk, McFarlane, & Weisaeth, 1996; Najavits, L.M., 2002; Friedman, 2005). Thus, it might be inferred that the daily anxiety and fear experienced by the guards of Abu Ghraib, in face of overwhelming ratio of guards to prisoners, that the assigned personnel experienced increased probability of PTSD development.

PTSD theorists (van der Kolk, McFarlane, & Weisaeth, 1996; Najavits, L.M., 2002; Friedman, 2005), and prominent organizations experienced in traumatic stress intervention, such as the National Organization for Victims Assistance (NOVA) and the International Critical Incident Stress Foundation (ICISF) argue that our lives evolve through a hierarchy of phases and needs.

Hierarchy of Needs

Abraham Maslow (1968), for example, proposed a pyramid of seven needs. Maslow argued that in progression to the pinnacle of self-actualization an individual needs to achieve satisfaction of each of the underlying six needs—psychological, safety, belongingness, esteem, cognitive, and aesthetic (see also Pervin, Cervone, John, 2005). Satisfaction of these needs is not, however, static. Instead, satisfaction is dynamic and relative to the individual. In other words, self-actualization in one individual may not meet the criteria of another. Additionally, the author argues that phases in an individual's life or changing circumstances may result in the need to reacquire any of the seven phases. In fact, one might ascend and descend the hierarchy of needs several times in his or her lifetime. This foundational thought is crucial in understanding the Abu Ghraib behavior. As the traumatic stress intensifies due to proximity or longevity, the level at which we operate regresses until it reaches the safety level.

Maslow proposed, in ascendance, deficit human needs could be expressed as physiological, safety, love or belonging, esteem. At the most primal level, Maslow argued people have an innate desire to survive. For example, given the choice between the needs of love and food, people generally tend to choose food. All other needs and desires are pushed to the back burner.

With physiological needs satisfied, individuals turn toward the need for safety. A remarkable observation is, in times of acute danger, safety needs may in fact take precedence over physiological needs. For example, in the days immediately following the liberation of Iraq, members of Shi'ite and Kurdish communities were seen to remain in secure areas without food, water, and electricity rather than venturing into areas held by Sunni insurgents despite the knowledge food and water existed in those areas.

The remaining two being needs consist of love and esteem. Love should not be confused with sexuality, but rather the unwavering innate need for human companionship and sense of belonging. Finally, esteem needs refers to the validation given to one's self by other people.

Group Adaptation

Individual behavior that is normal in the eyes of a larger body is nebulous at best, except to say that it exists within acceptable constraints for the sociocultural environment in which one finds himself or herself. Thus, subsequent evaluation of normal behavior must be assessed within the situation where it was exhibited.

Psychological and sociological textbooks (Pervin, Cervone, & John, 2005), suggest humans tend to evaluate their self-perception in context of their group affiliations. In their integrative self-schema model (ISSM), for example, Peterson, Stahlberg, and Dauenheimer (2000) proposed that self-schema elaboration directly influences search for, perception and processing of, and reaction to self-relevant information. Why is this phenomenon particularly important in the explanation of the Abu Ghraib Detention Facility guard behavior?

How individuals perceive themselves is directly influenced by group memberships. While numerous studies have demonstrated genetic predisposition (nature), the prevailing theory is that human personality and behavior are predominantly the result of a learned system of re-wards and punishment, which reflect the norms and values of one's sociocultural environment (nurture) (Pervin, Cervone, & John, 2005). One of the methods used by social psychologists and others concerned with human behavior to explain the formation of personality types is by ap-plying learning theory generalizations to the functional instrumental acts (operants) and positive or negative reinforcement consequences. The experiences of individuals resulting from membership in a particular group or culture are particularly relevant.

While minor variations may exist, behavioral theorists (Betz & Fry, 1995; Schlenker & Tedeschi; Fisher, 1990; Hudak, 1993) suggest members of a collective environment will adopt and demonstrate many of the characteristics and behaviors of the group. Analysis of prevailing group theory finds groups are more likely to polarize toward the extremes, take courses of ac-tion to promote the interests of the group in dissonance with one's morals, ethics , and values and perhaps to one's own detriment. This thought would seem to confirm prevailing military and gang organizational theory, in which one acts to preserve the safety afforded by the group en masse (i.e., "united we stand; divided we fall"). Interestingly, this is also the foundational basis of military basic training, in which individuality is systematically exorcised to instill a sense of the desirability of personal sacrifice to preserve the mutual survival of the unit. Group behavioral theorists also argue that groups are more likely to indulge in extreme attitudes and behavior. Fundamentally important to the study of Abu Ghraib is the belief that group mem-bers tend to believe group members are more likely to be correct than others. Consequently, because of these and other group biases, group members are far more apt to listen to one an-other than other people are. Unfortunately, group leaders then possess the ability to encourage individuals to act against their own interests to preserve or promote group identity.

Brehm, Kassin, and Fein (2005) suggest individuals conform to the norms of their sociocul-tural group for two reasons: 1) informational influence and, 2) normative influence. In the concept of informational influence, Brehm et al. (2005) argue that people conform because, as social individuals who want to satisfy our need to belong, we endeavor to be right. Thus, when others of our group confirm our judgment and behavior, we perceive that they must be right. Secondly, under the precept of normative influence, people conform because of the fear the consequences of being deviant. We often see this embodied in the Middle Eastern populations who fear Islamic retribution for aiding and abetting the Coalition. Brehm et al. (2005) describes the dilemma we face in our current efforts - public conformity versus private conformity. Whereas public conformity is viewed as a superficial change, in which the behavior of the audience apparently changes in assumed acceptance of views conflicting with their mental model, private conformity is viewed as the actual acceptance of conflicting rational information. Brehm et al. (2005) suggests that people often conform to peer pressure. It is, therefore, important to understand that people conform when peer pressure is intense and they are insecure individuals. Again, what we currently see in Iraq is the manifestation of this thought. Insurgents are endeavoring to demonstrate intense and overwhelming stimuli of grandiose proportions to increase fear in the population.

The question would then be, "Is transference of the trusted source possible during times of crisis?" Perhaps, the answer might be found in a common situation. Would, for example, an individual in counseling for alcoholism possess a greater tendency to seek the support of their family or fellow members of Alcoholics Anonymous (AA) during times of crisis? While, historically, the family unit may have been relied upon for general protection, the mere fact that alcoholism developed and persisted infers the family unit's inability to protect them from their desire for alcohol. Therefore, the individuals would logically seek the safety and security of their group membership.

Given the "small town" composition, this management style is typical in Reserve and National Guard units. However, adoption of group identity that is detrimental to individual identity is one of the key features of group affiliation; especially pervasive in the study of criminology. This concept would be especially true in view of the need for companionship in an unfamiliar environment.

As exemplified by the charge sheets indicting the members of this Reserve unit, this methodology was adopted not only in Abu Ghraib, but also perhaps as a unit methodology for survival. If one substitutes the word "conspired" in the charge sheets with the words "conferred" or "cooperated," the methodology becomes clear; the conspiracy was in actuality misguided loyalty to the team; the only tangible connection with familiar environment to which these Reservists were accustomed.

Subjective well-being

Moods, attitudes, emotions, and self-perception are found to fluctuate extensively over time and in response to one's situation and environment. Subjective well-being is one measure of the quality of life of both individuals and societies. In this context, how the members of our Armed Forces think and feel about themselves and their environment is essential to understanding the health of our fighting force.

The self-enhancement theory, for example, suggests people seek to protect or enhance their self-esteem when evaluating, accepting, or dismissing self-relevant information (Brown, 1986). Therefore, people tend to react more positively to feedback perceived as positive in reaction to some action or behavior. This premise was the basis of Festinger's theory of cognitive dissonance (Festinger, 1957). Consequently, the subjective well-being of the men and women of our armed forces is inextricably tied to Festinger's cognitive dissonance theory and the self-enhancement theory.

The awe effect

Seldom has the relationship between leader behavior and cohesion in natural groups been the subject of empirical study. Militarily, however, the relationship between combat unit leader behavior and unit cohesiveness and effectiveness has been extensively studied (Bartone & Kirkland, 1991). However, it might be argued that the forceful tactics used by SSGT Frederick and Corporal Graner, in a highly emotional environment to instill submissiveness, inspired the awe of their subordinates. Consequently, the subordinates emulated the behavior to earn the respect of these two individuals.

Investigative Findings

On January 31, 2004, MG Antonio M. Taguba was directed to conduct an informal investigation into the 800th MP Brigade's detention and internment operations. Specifically, MG Taguba was tasked to 1) inquire into all the facts and circumstances surrounding recent allegations of detainee abuse, specifically allegations of maltreatment at the Abu Ghraib Prison (Baghdad Central Confinement Facility (BCCF)); inquire into detainee escapes and accountability lapses as reported by Commander, Joint Task Force Seven (CJTF-7), specifically allegations concerning these events at the Abu Ghraib Prison; investigate the training, standards, employment, command policies, internal procedures, and command climate in the 800th MP Brigade, as appropriate; and make specific findings of fact concerning all aspects of the investigation, and make any recommendations for corrective action, as appropriate.

The results of the investigation were unmistakable; a clear pattern of blatant, wanton, and unquestionably sadistic abuses inflicted upon several of the detainees. The official report of investigation (Tabuga, 2004) suggested several members of the military police guard force in Tier 1-A of Abu Ghraib Prison had wantonly engaged in the systematic abuse of detainees in direct violation of the Uniformed Code of Military Justice (UC MJ) and several treaties regarding the fair treatment of prisoners of war.

Major General Taguba reported:

[B]etween October and December 2003, at the Abu Ghraib Confinement Facility (BCCF), numerous incidents of sadistic, blatant, and wanton criminal abuses were inflicted on several detainees…[S]ystemic and illegal abuse of detainees was intentionally perpetrated by several members of the military police guard force (372nd Military Police Company, 320thMilitary Police Battalion, 800th MP Brigade), in Tier (section) 1-A of the Abu Ghraib Prison (BCCF). Detailed witness statements substantiated the allegations of abuse…and the discovery of extremely graphic photographic evidence…In addition to the aforementioned crimes, there were abuses committed by members of the 325th MI Battalion, 205th MI Brigade, and Joint Interrogation and Debriefing Center (JIDC).

The Taguba Report indicted Staff Sergeant Ivan Frederick II, Specialist Charles A. Graner, Sergeant Javal Davis, Specialist Megan Ambuhl, Specialist Sabrina Harman, Specialist Jeremy Sivits, and Private Lynndie England with charges that included conspiracy, dereliction of duty, cruelty toward prisoners, maltreatment, assault, and indecent acts.

The Crystal Ball

Former Defense Secretary James Schlesinger argued that the abuses were the result of "free-lance activities" by the guards at the prison. Secretary of Defense Donald Rumsfeld issued a statement condemning the actions of the persons responsible, stating that their behavior was "wrong, cruel, brutal, indecent, and against American values and ... [he was] at a loss as to what kind of training could be provided to teach them" (Rumsfeld, 2004a). Consequently, charges of wrongdoing leveled against several members of the Military Intelligence (MI) and MP communities.

What tactics were permissible? On September 14, 2003, four months before ordering an investigation of the activities of Abu Ghraib, General Sanchez signed a memo (Sanchez, 2003) of authorized interrogation policies, which became effective immediately. These policies included: asking straight-forward questions; privileges or loss of privileges beyond those required by the Geneva Convention; enhancing the detainee's emotional love; enhancing the detainee's emotional hate; significantly increasing the detainee's fear; moderately increasing the detainee's fear; reducing the detainee's fear; increasing the detainee's ego; attacking the detainee's ego; invoking a feeling of futility; convincing of leading the detainee to believe the interrogator already knows the answer to the question; leading the detainee that their identity has been mistaken for someone else; repetitious questioning; convincing the detainee that the interrogator has a damning file that needs correction; good/bad interrogator; rapid fire questioning without the opportunity to answer; staring at the detainee in silence; situating the detainee in a different setting to increase/decrease comfort; dietary manipulation; sleep disturbance (not sleep deprivation); convincing the detainee that the interrogator is non-US; isolation; presence of muzzled working dog; sleep management; yelling, loud music, and light control; deception; and the use of stressful positions. General Sanchez explicitly concluded that the interrogators must be trained and under proper supervision when using these techniques. An unfortunate choice of wording is included on page 13 of General Sanchez' (2003) guidance, which states, "It is important that interrogators be provided reasonable latitude to vary techniques depending on detainee's culture, strengths, weaknesses, environment, extent of training in resistance techniques, as well as the urgency of obtaining information that the detainee is believed to have...205th MI BDE (Brigade) Commander is responsible for interrogation techniques involving physical contact" (Sanchez, 2003). However, none of the approved interrogation techniques allows the use of physical contact, leaving the reader with the inference that, while the guidance is explicated, "latitude" in methodology is permissible.

Unfortunately, the model for the events that unfolded during the early days had been presented in the early 1970s, yet was largely ignored in the hastily prepared facility. Were the occurrences at Abu Ghraib Prison Predictable? Several psychological and sociological theories provide predictive empirical data. The premier study that embodies the phenomenon described may be found in the 1971 Stanford Prison Experiment, in which Zimbardo, using a two-group posttest-only quasi-experimental design, studied the effects of a prison guard or inmate behavior in a simulated prison setting. In this study, a random sample of 24 students was selected from a population of 70 candidates. The group was randomly divided into two groups—guards or inmates—without any reference to discriminating factors. Former correctional personnel and inmates were retained to teach a course to the participants entitled, "Psychology of imprisonment."

The facility was constructed to closely resemble an actual detention facility environment, including no clocks, no view of the outside world, minimal sensory stimulation, effectively resulting in sensory deprivation. Additionally, to minimize distraction and diminish unnatural behavior, the capability to inconspicuously monitor and record the study was incorporated.

Procedurally, inmate processing was accomplished in a realistic manner. Blindfolded and in a state of mild shock from their surprise arrest by City Police, the inmates were driven from detention cells of the Palo Alto Police Department to the "Stanford County Jail" for further processing. Each inmate was systematically searched, stripped naked, and deloused. The objectives of this degradation process were two-fold. First, the inmates were humiliated to reduce individuality and self-awareness and to encourage submissiveness. Secondly, processing in such a manner ensured contraband, germs, and pests were not brought into the facility. To further induce submissiveness, the individuals were deprived of their individuality by being issued identical attire consisting of a smock, stocking cap, and rubber sandals. This removed any prior physical evidence of social status and effectively left the inmate with a feeling of emasculation. While some may argue a violation of human rights, this methodology has been used in military basic training for generations. Inmates were required to respond with assigned numbers instead of names. Chains on the ankles provided a 24-hour reminder of the extent of their circumstances.

As an elaboration of the social dominance theory, the guards invoked such physical labor as push-ups as a punitive measure. Guards were noted to place their feet on the backs of those performing push-ups, as well as sitting on their backs to establish social role relationships and create the guard dominance model. Post-experiment analysis revealed Zimbardo's experiment had created three distinct types of guards: 1) hostile, arbitrary and inventive in creation and execution of prisoner humiliation; 2) tough, but fair, guards who followed prison rules and; 3) "good guys" who emphasized and never punished the inmates.

An unexpected by-product of the Zimbardo experiment was guard solidarity. As the experiment evolved, the guards began to perceive the inmates not as actors, but rather as viable threats to their safety. This phenomenon greatly altered the experiment dynamics. The guards were noted to intensify their patterns of surveillance, dominance, and aggression. Every aspect of the inmate's life came under total domination of the guard force including bodily functions. Interestingly, a concluding finding was, despite random selection, guards were perceived by the inmates as being larger than life. Inmates believed individuals selected for guards were selected for their size. However, empirical data reveals no appreciable size differences in either group.

Conversely, methods were used to decrease inmate solidarity, including random cell rotation and the use of privilege to encourage intra-inmate distrust. Ex-felon consultants who advised that this was a highly effective tactic frequently employed to break inmate alliances and deflect attention away from the guards suggested this method. The result—successful distrust in a very confused inmate population. In elaboration of the effectiveness of such tactics, less than thirty-six hours into the experiment one inmate began to suffer from symptomatic acute emotional distress, disorganized thinking, and alternating periods of rage and crying. Labeled, chided as a weakling, and reminded that he agreed to participate; the participant began to engage in uncontrollable rage. Resultantly, the subject was released.

Within these experiments and studies, the theories of social construct, social dominance and gender role has seemingly been embodied. However, the contemporary military has added a new independent variable to the equation in the study of such behavior. Combat has historically been a masculine event, complete with the effects of male biological, sociological, and cultural adaptations. However, we have now placed the female gender in a traditionally male role in an effort to demonstrate diversity and equality. Unfortunately, while several studies have assessed the tangential characteristics such as intelligence and physical comparisons in a cross-gender environment, few if any have addressed the biological, sociological, and evolutionary factors in assumption of traditionally male roles occurring at the primal level—neither on the guard nor the prisoner level.

Courts-martial Results

Court-Martial charges against Staff Sergeant Ivan L. Frederick II, 38, alleged violations of UCMJ Articles 92, 93, 128, and 134, including conspiracy to maltreat detainees, dereliction of duty for negligently failing to protect detainees from abuse, cruelty and maltreatment; maltreating detainees by photographing them naked, posing for a photograph with a maltreated detainee; ordering detainees to strike each other; strike and assault detainees; and committing indecent acts. Under a plea agreement, he admitted to conspiracy, dereliction of duty, maltreatment of detainees, assault, and committing an indecent act to which he plead guilty, SSGT Frederick was sentenced on October 1, 2004 to a forfeiture of pay, Dishonorable Discharge, and a reduction in rank to Private (FindLaw, 2004c).

Widely considered to be the most culpable, Specialist Charles Graner, who had entered service on December 20, 2001, was found guilty on January 14, 2005 of all charges, including conspiracy to maltreat detainees, failing to protect detainees from abuse, cruelty, and maltreatment, as well as charges of assault, indecency, adultery, and obstruction of justice. He was sentenced to ten years in federal prison.

Frederick and Graner were the only two military members in the Military Police Unit with prior corrections experience. The remaining defendants had previously only held non-corrections experience.

Because of intense media scrutiny, the most publicly identifiable figure of the Abu Ghraib allegations was 21-year-old reservist Private First Class Lynndie England. Charged with nineteen counts of assault, conspiracy, improper conduct, and indecent acts. England's first trial in May 2005 resulted in a mistrial when testimony by Graner contradicted her guilty plea. On September 26, 2005, a jury of five male Army Officers found PFC England of six of the seven charges for which she was indicted, including conspiracy, maltreating detainees and committing an indecent act, convicted PFC England. She was acquitted on a second conspiracy count. Facing a maximum sentence of ten years, England was sentenced to three years confinement and a Dishonorable Discharge. During the course of England's Court-Martial, several of the fellow soldiers who had confessed to the alleged crimes testified to England's enjoyment at the abuse. The prosecutor argued England performed the acts for her "own sick humor" (Badger, 2005). Graphic photographs appeared to support the Prosecutor's contention England was a key participant in the abuse and conspiracy. Unfortunately, the above persons appear to have ignored several key psychological and criminological precepts provided by expert witnesses in their statements and conclusions.

Specialist Jeremy Sivits, 24, who enlisted in the Armed Forces on November 23, 1998, pled guilty to charges of conspiracy to maltreat detainees, and dereliction of duty for negligently failing to protect detainees from abuse, cruelty, and maltreatment. In exchange for his plea, Sivits was sentenced on May 19, 2004 by Special Court Martial to the maximum one-year sentence, demoted to Private and received a Bad Conduct Discharge (FindLaw, 2004b).

Specialist Roman Krol, Company A, 325th Military Intelligence Battalion, pled guilty February 1, 2005 to conspiracy and maltreatment of detainees at Abu Ghraib. Under a pretrial agreement, Krol, the sixth to be convicted, was sentenced to reduction in rank to Private, confinement for 10 months, and a Bad Conduct Discharge.

The seventh soldier to be convicted, Sergeant Jamal Davis was sentenced to reduction in rank to Private, six months confinement, and a bad conduct discharge on February 4, 2005 after pleading guilty to dereliction of duty, making false official statements and battery.

In exchange for his testimony against other defendants, Specialist Armin Cruz was sentenced on September 11, 2004 to eight months' confinement, reduction in rank to Private and a Bad Conduct Discharge.

Specialist Megan Ambuhl was reportedly present during sexually humiliating abuse, including the formation and photographing of a human pyramid of nude detainees. In mitigation, several detainees reportedly praised Ambuhl for treating them humanely and coming to the aid of a detainee who had difficulty breathing after being punched by another soldier. Ambuhl was convicted by Summary Court Martial on October 30, 2004 of dereliction of duty and sentenced to demotion to Private and loss of a half-month's pay for not reporting witnessed abuse. Ambuhl's attorney argued that she neglected to report the abuse because of the involvement of superiors and military intelligence personnel. Additional charges, including allegations of conspiracy, maltreatment, and indecent acts, against Ambuhl were dismissed in a pretrial agreement. The maximum sentence under Summary Court-Martial is thirty days. She was the third military police reservist and fourth U.S. soldier convicted in the Abu Ghraib prisoner abuse.

Specialist Sabrina Harmon, a former Pizza Store Manager from Lorton, Virginia who had joined the Army Reserves after 9/11 was photographed standing behind naked, hooded Iraqis stacked in a human pyramid. She was accused of photographing abuse, participating in sexual humiliation of naked prisoners, writing "rapist" on the leg of a detainee, who then was forced to pose naked with other prisoners, and intimidating a detainee by placing wires in the hands of a detainee and telling him he would be electrocuted if he fell off a box. After being convicted on six of seven counts, Specialist Harman was sentenced on May 17, 2005 to six months in prison and a Bad Conduct Discharge. If found guilty on all counts, Harman faced a maximum sentence of 5 years. During Harmon's court martial, her attorney, Frank Spinner, testified that prior to being activated for duty in the chaotic and overcrowded Abu Ghraib Detention Facility in Iraq, his client had virtually no prison guard experience and received virtually no training in her assigned duties. Also during her trial, Harmon's former Virginia roommate testified that in an October 2003 letter, Harmon has expressed distress and emotional dissonance regarding the occurrences of Abu Ghraib Prison. Did Harmon understand the difference between right and wrong? Clearly, the letter to her former roommate would indicate she did. However, the cognitive and emotional dissonances experienced arguably provide mitigating factors.

The 10th soldier convicted of prisoner abuse, Sergeant Michael Smith, was found guilty of using his unmuzzled barking and growling working dog, Marco, to mistreat a prisoner; mistreating two juvenile detainees at Abu Ghraib by harassing and threatening them with the dog; using his dog to make detainees soil themselves out of fear; and of failing to use his dog solely for authorized in such acts as terrify prisoners for amusement of other soldiers and allowing the dog to participate in the lewd acts of licking peanut butter off of a woman's (Specialist Jennifer Scala) chest and a man's genitalia. Smith was demoted to Private, and his monthly pay reduced by $750 for three months. Additionally, he was sentenced to 179 days confinement and a Bad Conduct Discharge. If found guilty on all counts, Smith faced a maximum penalty of more than 8 years in prison.

The 11th soldier, military dog handler, Sgt. Santos Cardona, 31, was found guilty of dereliction of duty and aggravated assault for allowing his dog to bark in the face of a kneeling detainee at the request of another soldier who was not an interrogator. He was acquitted him of other charges, including unlawfully having his dog bite a detainee and conspiring with another dog handler to frighten prisoners as a game. For his part in the Abu Ghraib mistreatment, He received 90 days hard labor without confinement and a reduction in rank for his actions.

After the investigative team of 26 persons responsible for investigating 44 specific instances of alleged mistreatment of detainees interviewed 170 personnel, and collected, catalogued and archived over 9,000 documents, the *Fay Report* (Fay, 2004) cited 27 persons as being responsible for abuse at Abu Ghraib Prison, including 23 soldiers from the military intelligence unit and four civilian contractors. While not directly involved in the mistreatment, five others with command responsibilities, including Col. Thomas Pappas, the 205th's Commanding Officer, and Lt. Col. Stephen Jordan, who commanded the prison interrogation center, were referred for possible disciplinary action.

While explicit discipline was meted out to the enlisted members in a swift, exacting manner, retribution was much more conflicted for the military officers. Of salience, Major General Tabuga told the Armed Services Committee that he did not find any *written* testimony that the military police members involved in the mistreatment were directed to do so. This assertion is problematic at many levels. Most visibly, General Taguba testified to the Senate Committee that General Sanchez, Commander of the troops in Iraq, had placed Abu Ghraib under control of the Military Intelligence Unit, not the Military Police Unit. However, Stephen Cambone, Under-Secretary of Defense for Intelligence, testified that the Military Intelligence Commander was only in charge of the military intelligence personnel, not military police personnel. Consequently, many on the Senate Committee opined that the chain of command received conflicting instructions regarding who was in charge.

Because of the Fay (2004) Report, five officers were referred for possible disciplinary actions. Following review, General Karpinski, Commanding Officer of the 800th Military Police Brigade, was further referred for disciplinary action. Lt. General Sanchez, Commander of U.S. Forces in Iraq at the time of the mistreatment, was cleared of wrongdoing. Further receiving no punishment was Major General (MGEN) Walter Wojdakowski, General Sanchez's former Intelligence Chief in Baghdad, MGEN Barbara Fast, and Colonel Mark Warren, General Sanchez's top legal advisor.

Colonel Karpinksi repeatedly insisted that it was military intelligence who gave instructions on interrogation techniques to military police members at Abu Ghraib. After being relieved of command, Colonel Karpinski was found guilty of dereliction of duty. The Review Board found that, despite Karpinski's performance of duty was seriously lacking, no action, or absence of action on her part specifically contributed to the mistreatment at Abu Ghraib. Resultantly, Karpinski received a reduction in grade.

A military hearing on the culpability of Lt. Col Jordan in October 2006 resulted in a call for court martial. Specifically, Jordan will answer for 12 charges; the most serious is allowing prisoners to be stripped nude, threatened with dogs, and be sexually humiliated. He is also accused of having twice-approving harsh interrogation techniques involving the use of dogs without seeking approval from the then-commanding officer Lt. General Sanchez. Exacerbating the seriousness of his actions, Jordan is accused of twice lying to investigators investigating the alleged mistreatment. Jordan retorts that the mission at Abu Ghraib was greatly influenced by the fact that Abu Ghraib was an extremely dangerous environment exacerbated by an explosive number of detainees. Jordan also asserted severe prison conditions, absence of security, and poor quality of life for troops at Abu Ghraib.

Finally, despite repeated findings of absence of culpability for the events at Abu h, Lt. General Sanchez was forced to retire from the Army in October 2006 after serving 33 years. While arguably slated to assume Commander of the U.S. Southern Command, Sanchez was denied any command opportunities; effectively ending his military career.

Conclusions

Much to the dismay of the George W. Bush Administration, the international media continues to demonstrate unprecedented adeptness at instilling or exacerbating anti-American sentiment throughout the world. This is especially true in the Arab countries of the Middle East. The ability to depict events from the most isolated spots in the world to virtually every television, magazine, and newspaper in the world in graphic, yet often myopic, detail almost instantaneously has proven to be problematic; a fact well known to our adversary, the al Qa'ida. Therefore, with thousands of Coalition troops on Arabic soil, the men and women are being placed in traumatic stress inducing environments and being expected to operate within the boundaries of a "normal" environment. Psychological and sociological studies, expert testimony, theories, and decades of research suggest this is not probable.

Placed in harm's way, frequently over tasked, undersupplied, and with many on their second and third deployments, the effects of fatigue and complex traumatic stress are seen to be taking a toll on the perception, cognition, and behavior of our fighting men and women. While combat stress units have been deployed to Iraq and Afghanistan, many cases of post-traumatic stress go undetected. One unfortunate aspect is the fact that the Operation Iraqi Freedom and Operation Enduring Freedom efforts are largely manned by Reserve and National Guard personnel, who are released to society upon return to the US without adequate psychological debriefing. The result is homicides, suicides, domestic dysfunction, and a host of comorbid, but seemingly disassociated disorders such as alcoholism.

Psychological and even military studies have repeatedly demonstrated that the most effective preventative measure is preparation. In the case of Abu Ghraib, the personnel were commanded by untrained personnel; uneducated in correctional facility and interrogation operations; inexperienced in unconventional warfare; undermanned; undersupplied; unable to communicate with the detainees; in constant apprehension and fear; and more importantly, not provided with oversight and stress management capabilities. The Fay Report (2004) found, while soldier interrogation training is adequate with respect to interrogation techniques and procedures for conventional warfare, it is far less suited to the realities of the Global War on Terrorism (GWOT) and Stability and Support Operations (SASO) and contract management. Despite the emphasis on the Geneva Conventions, it appeared clear from the results at Abu Ghraib and elsewhere that soldiers on the ground are confused about how they were to apply the Geneva Conventions and whether he or she has a duty to report violations of the conventions. Further, despite explicit instruction regarding certain types of interrogation techniques (Fay, 2004), the failure to list some techniques left a question of whether they were authorized for use without approval. By mid-October 2003, interrogation policy in Iraq had changed three times in less than 30 days. Various versions of each draft and policy were circulated among Abu Ghraib, further confusing the applicable policy. Fay (2004) suggested it was not always clear to JIDC officers what approaches required General Sanchez's approval, nor was the level of approval consistent with requirements in other commands.

Exacerbating the hypertension in the Abu Ghraib Complex were the fear existent in a combat zone, unfamiliarity and fear resulting from sociocultural diverseness, history of barbarism by the inmates, the relatively new introduction of females into a male dominated environment, and long-term exhaustion. The Stanford Prison Experiment provided empirical evidence beforehand to predict with utmost certainty, this chain of events would occur without conscious deliberation on the part of the participants.

Worldwide public outrage sparked by the Abu Ghraib photographs was exacerbated, if not generated, because it offended the Mental Eastern mental model of male dominance and ran contrary to the Western civilization's perception of femininity and gentility. However, it is important to reflect upon the fact that these brave females are being asked to serve as male equals in the traditionally heinous art of war, complete with the full range of emotions—fear, anger, and sadness, in which their femininity is stripped from them. The mere presence of females in a Middle Eastern combat situation would inevitably lead to intense emotional response on both sides of the battlefield.

While the actions of the convicted soldiers are considered egregious in a civilized society, it would be highly unlikely that even highly trained psychologists and mental health experts would be able to establish, *ex post facto*, the state of mind of the individuals involved. One of the few options that would have precluded this series of events would have been an objective observer or objective observer, not associated with the Abu Ghraib Facility monitoring the guard activity and state of mental health. Again, the precedence for this assertion is well elaborated in the Stanford Prison experiment. However, the significance of this assertion would not have become known without the revelation of the detrimental effects of not providing for the physical and mental well-being of the guards of Abu Ghraib.

Alan L. Hensley can be reached for comment by writing to **DrHensley1@aol.com**

References

Ajzen, I. & Fishbein, M. (1980). *Understanding the attitudes and predicting social behavior.* Englewood Cliffs, New Jersey: Prentice-Hall Inc.

American Psychiatric Association. (2000). *Diagnostic and statistical manual of mental disorders* (4th ed., text revision). Washington, DC: Author.

Badger, T.A. (2005). *England convicted of six of the seven counts.* Retrieved September 26, 2005 from http://hosted.ap.org/dynamic/stories/p/prisoner_abuse_england?site=kgw&template =default&section=home

Betz, B., & Fry, W.R. (1995). The role of group schema in the selection of influence attempts. *Basic and Applied Social Psychology, 16*(3), 351-365.

Bless, H., Clore, G. L., Schwarz, N., Golisano, V., & Rabe, C. (1996). Mood and the use of scripts: Does a happy mood really lead to mindlessness? *Journal of Personality and Social Psychology, 71,* 665-679.

Bless, H., Schwarz, N., & Wieland, R. (1996). Mood and the impact of category membership and individuating information. *European Journal of Social Psychology, 26,* 935-959.

Bowman, C. H., & Fishbein, M. (1978). Understanding public reaction to energy proposals: An application of the Fishbein model. *Journal of Applied Social Psychology, 9,* 319-340.

Brehm, S.S., Kassin, S., & Fein, S. (2005) *Social psychology* (6th ed.). Boston: Houghton Mifflin.

Brown, J. D. (1986). Evaluations of self and others: Self-enhancement biases in social judgments. *Social Cognition, 4,* 353-376.

Coie, J. D., Underwood, M., & Lochman, J. E. (1991). Programmatic intervention with aggressive children in the school setting. In D. J. Pepler, & K. H. Rubin (Eds.), *The development and treatment of childhood aggression* (pp. 389– 410). Hillsdale, NJ: Lawrence Erlbaum Associates.

Crick, N. R., & Dodge, K. A. (1994). A review and reformulation of social information-processing mechanisms in children's social adjustment. *Psychological Bulletin, 115,* 74-101.

Cummings, W.H. & Venkatesan, M. (1976). Cognitive dissonance and consumer behaviour: A review of the evidence. *Journal of Marketing Research, 13* (3), 303-308.

Dodge, K. A. (1980). Social cognition and children's aggressive behavior. *Child Development, 51,* 162-170.

Dodge, K. A., & Newman, J. P. (1981). Biased decision making processes in aggressive boys. *Journal of Abnormal Psychology, 90,* 375-379.

Dodge, K., Petit, G., McClaskey, & Brown, M. (1986). Social Competence in Children. *Monographs of the Society for Research in Child Development, 51*(2), 213.

Dodge, K. A., & Tomlin, A. (1987). Cue utilization as a mechanism of attributional bias in aggressive children. *Social Cognition, 5,* 280-300.

Engel, C.C. (2005). *Congressional testimony on posttraumatic stress syndrome.* Retrieved February 13, 2006 from
http://www.highbeam.com/library/wordDoc.doc?docid=1P1:111661973

Fay, G.R. (2004). AR 15-6 investigation of the Abu Ghraib Detention Facility and *205th Military Intelligence Brigade* (U). Retrieved November 6, 2006 from
http://fl1.findlaw.com/news.findlaw.com/hdocs/docs/dod/fay82504rpt.pdf.

Festinger, L. (1957). *A theory of cognitive dissonance.* Stanford, CA: Stanford University Press.

FindLaw, (2004a) *Preferred Charges against Corporal Charles Graner.* Retrieved December 6, 2004 from http://news.findlaw.com/hdocs/docs/iraq/graner51404chrg.html

FindLaw, (2004b) *Preferred Charges against Specialist Jeremy C. Sivits.* Retrieved December 6, 2004 from http://news.findlaw.com/hdocs/docs/iraq/sivits50504chrg2.html

FindLaw, (2004c) *Court-Martial Charges against Staff Sergeant Ivan L. Frederick, II.* Retrieved December 6, 2004 from http://news.findlaw.com/hdocs/docs/iraq/ifred32004chrg.html

Fisher, R.J. (1990). The social psychology of intergroup and international conflict resolution. New York: Springer Verlag.

Friedman, M.J. (2005). *Congressional testimony on posttraumatic stress syndrome.* Retrieved February 13, 2006 from http://www.highbeam.com/library/wordDoc.doc?docid=1P1:111661971

Goldenhar, L. M., & Connell, C. M. (1993). Understanding and predicting recycling behavior: An application of the theory of reasoned action. *Journal of Environmental Systems, 22,* 91-103.

Haney, C., Banks, C., & Zimbardo, P. (1973). Interpersonal dynamics in a simulated prison. *International Journal of Criminology and Penology, 1,* 69-97.

Hensley, A. L. (2004). *Why good people go bad: A case for the defendants indicted in the Abu Ghraib abuse investigation.* Unpublished manuscript provided to the Area Defense Counsel for use as a defense framework.

Hudak, M.A. (1993). Gender schema theory revisited: men's stereotypes of American women. *Sex Roles, 28*(5-6), 279-293.

Jones, R. E. (1990). Understanding paper recycling in an institutionally supportive setting: An application of the theory of reasoned action. *Journal of Environmental Systems, 19,* 307-321.

Karpinski, J. (2005). *One woman's army: The Commanding General of Abu Ghraib tells her story.* New York: Hyperion.

Maslow, A. H. (1968). *Toward a psychology of being* (2nd ed.). New York: Van Nostrand Reinhold.

Moghaddam, F. M., & Marsalla, A. J. (ed.) (2004). *Understanding terrorism: Psychological roots, consequences, and interventions.* Washington, D.C.: American Psychological Association.

Najavits, L.M. (2002). *Seeking safety: A treatment manual for PTSD and substance abuse.* New York: Guilford.

Oliver, R.L. (1997). *Satisfaction: A behavioral perspective on the consumer.* New York: McGraw-Hill.

Pervin, L. A., Cervone, D., & John, O. P. (2005). *Personality: Theory and research* (9th ed.). New York: Wiley.

Pinker, S. (2002). *The blank slate: The modern denial of human nature.* New York: Penguin.

Sanchez, R. S. (2003). *CTJF-7 interrogation and counter-resistance policy.*

Schlenker, B.R., Tedeschi, J.T. (1972). Interpersonal attraction and the exercise of coercive and reward power. *Human Relations 15,* 427-439.

Strasser, S. (2004). *The Abu Ghraib investigations.* New York: Public Affairs.

Taguba, A. (2004). *Article 15-6 Investigation of the 800th Military Police Brigade.* Retrieved December 7, 2004 from http://www.globalsecurity.org/intell/library/reports/2004/800-mp-bde.htm

The Hutchinson Encyclopedia, (2003). Cognitive Dissonance. Retrieved March 28, 2006 from http://www.highbeam.com/library/wordDoc.doc?docid=1P1:100126480.

Van der Kolk, B.A., McFarlane, A.C., & Weisaeth, L. (Ed.) (1996). *Traumatic stress.* New York: Guilford.

Wabha, M. A., & Bridwell (1976). Maslow reconsidered: A review of research on the hierarchy theory. *Organizational Behavior and Human Performance, 15,* 212-240.

Zoroya, G. (2005). *1 in 4 Iraq vets ailing on return.* Retrieved November 28, 2005 from http://www.usatoday.com/news/world/iraq/2005-10-18-troops-side_x.htm

Zimbardo, P. (2004*). Stanford prison experiment: A simulation study of the psychology of imprisonment conducted at Stanford University.* Retrieved on September 27, 2005 from http://www.prisonexp.org/

About the Author

Alan Hensley is a retired 25-year national-level Intelligence Officer with extensive experience in special operations, counter-insurgency operation, and intelligence collection operations in hostile environments. He possesses a BS in Healthcare Management, BS in Information Systems Management, an MS in Criminal Justice, and is currently in the dissertation phase of Capella University's Human Services PhD program, specializing in research and treatment of PTSD. He has extensive experience in psychological operations (PSYOP), human intelligence collection, cryptologic operation, and traumatic stress intervention. He is highly active in Iowa's Operation Enduring Families, participating in pre-, peri-, and post-deployment counseling of National Guard men and women serving in Operation Enduring Freedom and Operation Iraqi Freedom (OEF/OIF) and their families. He is also active in the National Organization for Victims' Assistance (NOVA), Nebraska and Iowa organizations counseling victims of childhood sexual abuse, and is the Mills County, Iowa Victims of Domestic Violence and Sexual Assault Advocate Coordinator, giving him far-reaching experience in PTSD development and predisposition.

Life After a Terrorist Attack:
Resiliency of Israeli Suicide Bombing Victims

Thom Curtis, Ph.D. and Joshua Faudem

Abstract

Joshua Faudem and Thom Curtis, Ph.D. made a combined presentation on November 9, 2006 at the 2006 Rocky Mountain Disaster Mental Health Conference in Casper, Wyoming. Curtis introduced Faudem and then provided some historical background on suicide bombing in Israel.

Suicide Bombing in Israel

Thom Curtis, Ph.D., a sociologist at the University of Hawaii-Hilo introduced the topic of the Israeli population's resiliency during years of suicide terrorist attacks. He described observations based on interviews conducted during research visits to Israel in February and September of 2006.

Curtis reported that there were over 165 major terrorism attacks on civilians in Israel during the period of 2000-2006. These attacks resulted in 999 noncombatant deaths and almost 5,000 wounded. Thirty-three of the attacks were on busses or bus stops resulting in 288 dead. Twenty were on malls or markets with 80 dead. Another 80 died in eight attacks on restaurants. Five bombings of clubs and discos accounted for 69 deaths.

Israel has a population of 6,276,883. Curtis statistically compared the terrorism deaths in Israel since 2000 to the deaths the United States experienced on September 11, 2001. The ratio of deaths on September 11 amounted to ten deaths for every one million American citizens. Since 2000, Israel has experienced 159 terrorism-caused deaths per million citizens. On September 11, there was one death for every 100,000 Americans. In Israel, there has been one terrorism-caused death for every 6,238 citizens since 2000.

Curtis then introduced Joshua Faudem. He is an Israeli filmmaker who was working on a documentary about Mike's Place, an English language restaurant and bar in Tel Aviv that was noted for its friendliness, good music and which served as a respite from the constant stress of living in a city experiencing a siege of terrorism. While he was filming interviews shortly after midnight on April 30, 2003, a suicide bomber exploded in the doorway of Mike's Place. Two musicians and a waitress, who was a central focus of the documentary, were killed. The film's American producer, Jack Baxter was seriously injured.

Faudem and his assistant, Pavla Fleischer, from the Czech Republic were filming the band when the explosion occurred. Despite their own injuries and shock, they kept the cameras rolling during the immediate aftermath and throughout the next week as the owners and staff of Mike's Place struggled to deal with the shock of the bombing, the loss of their friends and reopen the club for a memorial service.

Faudem introduced the documentary, *Blues by the Beach*. The film earned the 2006 Pierre Salinger Award for Documentary Filmmaking at the New York Film Festival and was also recognized as the Conflict and Resolution Award winner at the Hampton Film Festival. It is a juxtaposition of tranquil footage shot before the attack with traumatic scenes of the bombing's aftermath and the heroic recovery attempted by the Mike's Place family.

Blues by the Beach

Blues by the Beach is a 75-minute long documentary film. It begins as the story of an exceptional respite from the daily terrorist attacks of the Second Intafada and morphs into parallel stories of survival and resiliency exhibited by both the employees of Mike's Place and the film crew.

On the evening of April 29, 2003, Jack Baxter an American documentary producer and investigative journalist arrived at Mike's Place a restaurant and bar next to the American Embassy in Tel Aviv, Israel. With him were his film crew, including Israeli-American director, Joshua Faudem, and videographer, Pavla Fleischer, from the Czech Republic. They were there to make a documentary about the place that advertises itself as, "an island of sanity in a region torn apart by conflict." Israel and its Palestinian neighbors were in the third year of the five year "*Second Intifada*[1]." There had been 304 terrorist attacks against Israelis prior to that evening and many similar businesses had been closed because of the danger of suicide bombers, but Mike's Place was different. It was a place that catered to music lovers of all ethnic and religious persuasions. The Mike's Place website features an open invitation: "For those wishing to put their differences aside, the bar has always provided a relaxed haven to enjoy live music and good company."

While Hebrew is the primary language of Israel, English is the custom at Mike's Place. In fact, the opportunity to converse in English may entice as many customers as the blues and rock. Immigrants from throughout the former British Empire, American expatriates and locals who simply want to converse in English enjoy the American style menu and music.

The film crew was videotaping the band between interviews with employees and patrons. They had already recorded many hours of video with the staff and were hoping to capture the spirit of club. Everyone thought they were capturing a normal, busy weeknight at Mike's Place.

Avi Tabib, the bouncer, was in his usual place in front of restaurant shortly after midnight the next morning. The music was good and so was business for a weekday. A customer with a British accent tried to cut ahead of the line waiting to enter the restaurant. Something about him caused Avi to feel uncomfortable and he told the man to move along.

The man Avi confronted was later identified as Asif Muhammad Hanif, 22, a British citizen of Pakistani descent. He was accompanied by Omar Khan Sharif, 27, who had also been born in Great Britain. Dominique Hass, 29, a French Waitress who had been featured in previously-taped interviews came out of the restaurant to ask Avi a question, but realized he was distracted by the young man at the edge of the sidewalk. She stepped aside and Hanif suddenly

---

[1] The Second Intifada or Al Asqa Intifada was a wave of clashes between Palestinian Arabs and Israelis that started in September 2000. On September 28, 2000, an Israeli opposition leader who would subsequently become the country's Prime Minister, Ariel Sharon, visited the Al Asqa mosque compound of the Temple Mount in the Old City of Jerusalem. The area is considered the third most revered-site in Islam and the Jewish politician's presence was met by protests and rioting among Palestinians began following day. Suicide bombings soon became a common Palestinian tactic of the Second Intifada. Official estimates put the death toll at 1,001 Israelis or visitors to Israel and 2,124 Palestinians.

pushed forward. As Avi crouched to tackle the man, a blast wave lifted off the ground and threw him through the windows into the restaurant.

When the smoke cleared, Avi was unconscious under a table, his body crushed and bleeding. He suffered critical internal injuries, broken bones in the skull, the jaw, hands, and shoulders, broken teeth, torn ligaments and muscles, and a torn eardrum. Additionally, he had burns all over his body, including his vocal cords and lungs. In the rubble, over sixty people were injured. Some including, Jack (the Producer), were injured very seriously. Dominique, the French waitress, was dying. Musicians Ran Baron, 23, and Yanai Weiss, 46, were dead.

As the smoke of the blast clears, *Blues by the Beach* shifts to tell the parallel stories of courage. The first story is about the Mike's Place family as it struggles to deal with its loses and to reopen the club in time for Israel's Memorial Day one week after the blast. The second story is of the efforts by Joshua and Pavla to document Mike's Place as it recovered from the attack while dealing with their personal brush with death and the subsequent demise of their romantic relationship.

Blues by the Beach captures the emotional and psychological aftermath of a suicide bombing in an unprecedented manner. Candid discussions among the survivors were recorded as they talked about their responses, struggled to make sense of the experience and support each other. The film does an excellent job representing a wide range of responses and recovery mechanisms, healthy and unhealthy, employed by the various participants.

After viewing the video, Faudem and Curtis answered questions from conference participants. The focus of the discussions was on the resiliency of Israelis in general and those who survived the bombing of Mike's Place in particular. Faudem discussed how his personal recovery has progressed since the film was completed. He also described the ongoing impact of the attack on other survivors including the producer of the film, Jack Baxter.

Curtis described his interviews with survivors, focusing specifically on Avi, the bouncer. After a lengthy hospitalization, Avi awakened from a coma and eventually returned to Mike's Place as a bouncer. Though still suffering emotional and physical scars from the attack, he has graduated from college, married, had a baby and started his own security company. He is still the only security guard in Israel to have confronted a suicide bomber and survived the blast.

About the Author

Thom Curtis, Ph.D., is an Associate Professor at the University of Hawaii at Hilo where he focuses on terrorism and disaster psychology/sociology. He has participated in numerous disaster responses from Guam to New York and served as a consultant to government and private agencies involved in disasters. Over the two years, he has traveled across the Atlantic three times to conduct terrorism related research in Europe, the Middle East and North Africa. While his primary focus is on the social and psychological attributes of terrorists, he has also examined the resiliency of direct and indirect survivors of terrorism attacks in Israel, Europe and the U.S. His recent work includes journal articles titled, "Child Abuse in the Wake of Natural Disasters" and "Fatal Aviation Accidents in Rural Communities: Response Preparation Strategies and presentations titled "The Path to Jihad: Recruitment of U.S. Citizens by Islamist Organizations" and "Native Hawaiian Perceptions of Violence as a Means to Attain Sovereignty". He also edited the book, *Hawaii Remembers September 11*. He is a licensed Marriage and Family Therapist and American Red Cross Disaster Mental Health Instructor.

For further information, please contact:
Thom Curtis, Ph.D. thomc@hawaii.edu
Department of Sociology
University of Hawaii-Hilo
200 West Kawili Street
Hilo, Hawaii 96720

Joshua Faudem was born in Detroit MI in 1975 His interests include World history, world politics, photography, visual art/painting/film, Psychology and music. He was a member of Israel's 93'-98' national softball team. Joshua education included 88'-92': Golda Meir High School, Jerusalem, Israel; 92'-94': School of Performing Arts Theatre Department, Jerusalem Israel;99'-02': Academy of Performing Arts FAMU (Film, TV & Photography) In Prague. His Projects/short films include: 1998 " In My Comfortable Shoes" 1999, " Full Service" 2000, "The Man Who Had Enough" 2000 ", The Sound of Tolerance" 2002, "Jerusalem Pride", Projects/Feature Length Films include: 2001 "A Will To Dance" documentary 2004, "Blues By The Beach" documentary 2004, "Russki Battalion" documentary MILITARY SERVICE: 1994-1997 - First sergeant in the 50th regiment/airborne, IDF (Israeli Defense Forces) EMPLOYMENT: 1997-98 Nursery school teacher at Kibbutz Zellim, Negev, Israel. 1998 Commercial fisherman, Monterey, CA. 1999 Assistant photographer, Lighthouse Productions, New York. 2000-01 Director, " I Will To Dance" Axman productions, Prague, Czech Rep. 2002 assistant producer, associated producers, Toronto, on the film "JAMES" for discovery channel. 2003-04 Director, " Russki Battalion", Globus Group, Tel Aviv, Israel 2004-05 Director, "Blues By The Beach", Pax Americana, New York, USA 2006 Assistant director, The Third Temple Trilogy, FPAD Productions, Tel Aviv, Israel 2006 Director, "Sounds of Music from Ramallah", FPAD Productions, Tel Aviv, Israel

Role of Culture and Cultural Sensitivity in Disaster Response:

A Roundtable Discussion

Alan L. Hensley, PhD Candidate, BCETS, FAAETS

During the Rocky Mountain Disaster Mental Health Conference, a tabletop discussion endeavored to understand the sociocultural implications of the Diagnostic and Statistical Manual of Mental Disorders, Fourth Edition, Text Revision (American Psychiatric Association, 2000) in a multicultural environment. Specifically addressed was the assertion that mental diagnosis of included mental illnesses and comorbid disorders largely reflect the Western European North American Caucasian population. Addressed was the assertion that cross-cultural, child, and adolescent behavior is largely conflicted and frequently misdiagnosed because of the rigidity of criteria of the DSM-IV-TR.

In attempting to apply the DSM-IV-TR in relationship to multi-cultural environments potentially encountered in disaster response, several assertions and assumptions were made. The first assumption asserts that the DSM-IV-TR's (APA, 2000) diagnostic system is based on the assumption that mental illness reflects facts about people struggling in the world. A reading of the introduction, however, finds that disorders were created based on reports of complaints and functional disturbances, with arbitrary distinctions being drawn between types of dysfunction. After these distinctions were made, the clusters of symptoms were given a name. Thus, the depth and breadth of mental dysfunction is broadly categorized, leading to the possibility of misinterpretation and misdiagnosis. Overall, it appears that looking at problems within the current all-or-nothing categorical system creates false dichotomies and is not empirically supported. Examining individual differences in psychological phenomena improves on the current dichotomous categorical system.

Assumption 2 of the workgroup asserted that diagnostic labels promote understanding. Reflecting the assertions of speakers earlier, as currently established, DSM-IV-TR categories describe only the negative aspects of the person's life and do not elucidate human strength or the process of human change (Barone et al., 1997). Thus, the problem arises that practitioners, rather than attempting to understand the diversity of the population or the richness of the client's strengths and coping mechanisms, is constrained to merely relegate the individual into a negative category, which in turn results in stigmatization and resentment. Such static negative labeling can create stereotypical expectations that influence how professionals conceptualize and interact with individuals, as well as how these labeled individuals may think about themselves.

Assumption 3 asserts that DSM-IV diagnosis and treatment are correlated. Specifically, negative labels lead the clinician to having a set of negative expectations. Conversely, the individuals attributed to the negative labels are likely to respond in a stereotypically expected manner.

The workgroup was comprised of representatives from various disciplines in the United States, United Kingdom, and a representative from the Northern Arapahoe Tribe of Wyoming. Thus, a broad diversity existed in sociocultural, religious, and spiritual perspectives. In discussion, it was generally agreed upon that looking at problems within the current all-or-nothing categorical system creates false dichotomies and is not empirically supported. Rather, the participants reached the consensus that although all people experience problems, these difficulties are best represented as occurring on a continuum (Barone, Maddux, & Snyder, 1997) in which generalization becomes problematic.

The following discussion reflects not only upon problematic issues when addressing children and adolescents, but also in relationship to the nearly 8,000 children of the Northern Arapahoe Tribe of Wyoming (Sage, 2006). Allison Sage, MSW, the leader of the workgroup, *The Role of Culture and Cultural Sensitivity in Disaster Response,* is a member of the Northern Arapahoe Tribe and is currently serving as the Tribal Liaison for the Governor of the State of Wyoming to the Northern Arapahoe Tribal Council. Discussed were issues directly related to applying the DSM-IV-TR to issues frequently seen among the children of the Northern Arapahoe Tribe. Frequently, the children are diagnosed as:

AXIS I:	314.00 Attention Deficit/Hyperactivity Disorder, Predominantly Inattentive
	312.81 Conduct Disorder, Childhood Onset Type
	313.81 Oppositional Defiant Disorder
	315.00 Reading Disorder
AXIS II:	301.7 Antisocial Personality Disorder
	301.82 Avoidant Personality Disorder
	301.6 Dependent Personality Disorder
	318.0 Mental Retardation

Axis I disorders (American Psychiatric Association, 2000) reflect clinical disorders or other conditions that may be a focus of clinical attention. Axis II disorders, alternatively reflect personality disorders or mental retardation, such as paranoia, schizoid personality disorder, schizotypical personality disorder, antisocial personality disorder, borderline personality disorder, histrionic personality disorder, narcissistic personality disorder, avoidant personality disorder, dependent personality disorder, obsessive-compulsive personality disorder, other personality disorders, and mental retardation.

Discussion with Allison Sage on November 10, 2006 at the Rocky Mountain Region Disaster Mental Health Conference reflects, however, application of the DSM-IV-TR proves problematic in view of the endemic nutritional problems existing on the Wind River Reservation. Specifically, reservation children frequently only receive regular meals at school in the morning and at lunch. Often the children do not expect to receive an evening meal for a myriad of reasons including the lack of food at home, the absence of anyone to prepare the meal, the lack of transportation to buy food and several other similar reasons. A reading of Marshak (2006) reveals that this situation is not unique to the Wind River Reservation. Marshak (2006) relates the story of Paul LaRoche, founder of the Native American musical group, *Brule'* and his journey to understand his Lakota heritage in Lower Brule, South Dakota

Additionally, dysfunctional home life, combined with nutritional difficulty results in conduct disorders and the inability to concentrate. This assertion is well grounded in Maslow's Hierarchy of Needs, which suggests physiological needs are pivotal to all other needs; left unsatisfied, higher needs cannot be met. Consequently, that which might be diagnosed as ADHD might, in fact, be understood in the application of the biopsychosocial model (i.e., the inability to concentrate because of hunger). Left unabated, however, the consequences might in fact evolve into more pervasive conduct disorder.

An additional confounding variable related by Allison Sage on November 10, 2006 rests within the spirituality of Native American beliefs. Among the Northern Arapahoe, it is a spiritual belief that for the first ten years of life, children are angels. Failure to provide for, nurture, and otherwise care for these angels will result in the children being taken from the family. During this period, strong emphasis is placed upon spirituality. Consequently, lacking understanding of such beliefs, the practitioner is likely to diagnose psychoticism.

Conclusion: Both Axis I and Axis II disorders and dysfunctions are problematic when addressing children in view of the circumstances discussed. First, children, as expressed by Erikson's stages of development (Erikson, 1968, 1982), are evolving. Consequently, permanency of perceived disorders and dysfunctions are not assured. Secondly, while the DSM-IV-TR provides a basic framework for categorization of mental health disorder and dysfunction, sociocultural and spiritual understanding is imperative to application of the criteria.

About the Author

Alan Hensley is a retired 25-year national-level Intelligence Officer with extensive experience in special operations, counter-insurgency operation, and intelligence collection operations in hostile environments. He possesses a BS in Healthcare Management, BS in Information Systems Management, an MS in Criminal Justice, and is currently in the dissertation phase of Capella University's Human Services PhD program, specializing in research and treatment of PTSD. He has extensive experience in psychological operations (PSYOP), human intelligence collection, cryptologic operation, and traumatic stress intervention. He is highly active in Iowa's Operation Enduring Families, participating in pre-, peri-, and post-deployment counseling of National Guard men and women serving in Operation Enduring Freedom and Operation Iraqi Freedom (OEF/OIF) and their families. He is also active in the National Organization for Victims' Assistance (NOVA), Nebraska and Iowa organizations counseling victims of childhood sexual abuse, and is the Mills County, Iowa Victims of Domestic Violence and Sexual Assault Advocate Coordinator, giving him far-reaching experience in PTSD development and predisposition.

References

American Psychiatric Association. (2000). Diagnostic and statistical manual of mental disorders (4th ed., text rev.). Washington, DC: Author.

Barone, D., Maddux, J., & Snyder, C. R. (1997). The social cognitive construction of difference and disorder. In D. Barone, J. Maddux, & C. R. Snyder (Eds.), Social cognitive psychology: History and current domains (pp. 397-428). New York: Plenum.

Erikson, E.H. (1968). *Identity: Youth and Crisis.* New York: Norton.

Erikson, E.H. (1982). *The life cycle completed.* New York: W. W. Norton.

Marshak, B. (2006). Hidden heritage: The story of Paul LaRoche. Minneapolis, MN: Beaver's Pond Press.

Culture & Ethics in the Eye of the Storm: Engaging Katrina Survivors in Pennsylvania

Kenneth Glass, Ph.D. and Tasha Graves, M.S.

Philadelphia, PA

Tommy Davis, Ph.D., Suziliene Board, Psy.D., and Marquita Williams, M.A. are contributors

"Probably the worst catastrophe, or set of catastrophes, in the country's history"

—Michael Chertoff, Homeland Security Secretary

The Devastation of Hurricane Katrina

Hurricane Katrina is frequently referred to as the most devastating natural disaster in recent United States history. The storm was relentless in intensity and battered New Orleans and much of the Gulf region. Describing the aftermath of Hurricane Katrina, Homeland Security Secretary Michael Chertoff was quoted calling it "Probably the worst catastrophe, or set of catastrophes, in the country's history" (CNN.com).

The impact of Hurricane Katrina, of course, is seen in human and physical terms. For sheer size, Hurricane Katrina is reported by Federal disaster authorities to have covered 90,000 square miles. To understand its scope, 90, 000 square miles is roughly the size of the United Kingdom. Financially, the cost damage from Katrina is estimated to be nearly double the cost of the previously most expensive storm. The latest estimate of the financial toll is at $81.2 billion. (Knabb, et al.,2005).

Structurally, the City of New Orleans was devastated and will require years to rebuild. Several estimates concluded that up to 80% of New Orleans was under water. In some sections, water was 20 feet deep (Fox News/Associated Press 2005; Department of Homeland Security). The Army Corps of Engineers spent 53 days pumping out an estimated 250 billion gallons of water in New Orleans. The economic damage includes interruptions of the oil supply, the Gulf Coast's highway infrastructure, and commodity exports.

Naturally, the most distressing outcome of Katrina is the toll it took on families. No less than 800,000 people were forced to live outside of their homes—the largest displacement of people since the great Dust Bowl migrations of the 1930s. Basic living necessities were also in short supply. For example, Hurricane Katrina left an estimated three million people without electricity. Finally, the confirmed death toll (total of direct and indirect deaths) stood at 1,836, mainly from Louisiana (1,577) and Mississippi (238). In addition, 705 people remain categorized as missing in Louisiana, so this number is not final even a year after the storm (Louisiana Department of Health and Hospitals, 2006)(Krupa, 2006).

"People are without food, without a decent place to live, without medicine. We cannot stand idly by and allow this suffering to continue. We have a moral responsibility to do something. I concluded it was time for action."

—John Street, Mayor of Philadelphia

Responding to Hurricane Katrina

The response to Hurricane Katrina remains one of the largest search and rescue operations in United States history. Approximately 58,000 National Guard personnel were activated to deal with the storm's aftermath, with troops coming from all 50 states. (Phillips, 2005). The Coast Guard deployed hundreds of air and boat crews to rescue more than 24,273 people. In fact, the Coast Guard devoted more than 40 % of its helicopter fleet to support rescue operations. 28 Urban Search & Rescue teams nationwide were placed into action to assist with response and rescue efforts in the Gulf region. FEMA deployed 6,300 personnel, including nurses and physicians, who cared for more than 165,000 people in the weeks following the storm. The Department of Defense also activated volunteer members of the Civil Air Patrol. Estimates suggest that Katrina rescue efforts resulted in a range from 24,135 to 33,735 lives saved and 9,409 evacuated. For the entire region, the Bush Administration has sought at least $110 billion for repairs and reconstruction in the region (Sheikh, 2005) (Congressional Research Service, 2006).

Beyond the Federal and Gulf Region governments, private organizations have contributed to rescue and post rescue efforts. Reports estimate over $3.5 billion in cash and in-kind donations. Five charities accounted for more than 85% of the money raised: the Red Cross ($2.1 billion); the Salvation Army ($365 million); Catholic Charities USA ($146 million); the Bush-Clinton Katrina Fund ($129 million) and Habitat for Humanity ($122 million) (DHS.com).

> "This could be the greatest natural disaster in our country's history. We need a response commensurate with that. We have made a commitment and we mean it. Send those victims here now. This City — the City of Brotherly Love — will respond."
>
> —John Street, Mayor of Philadelphia

The Mayor Calls

Disaster mental health work has steadily evolved in the past 20 years. The service has largely focused on providing intervention and support to a variety of responders to crises and emergencies. Responders include fire personnel, police officers, clergy, medics and others. Essentially, the aim of the intervention is to "help the helpers" process and digest emotional and psychological reactions to tragedy.

Exposure to tragedy affects individuals, regardless of their role, in significant, lasting, and in some cases, damaging ways. Trauma, one potential outcome of exposure to tragedy, manifests in several symptoms. When coalesced and of required intensity, it takes the form of Post-Traumatic Stress Disorder. PTSD is a serious disorder that can have ongoing consequences for a person. While PTSD is one serious result of exposure to a trauma, reactions to trauma that do not add up to PTSD are also debilitating for people. The risk for Responders is evident in this area.

Generally speaking, the influence of trauma is largely defined in psychiatric symptoms and syndromes. The symptoms include flashbacks, recurring nightmares, fear, etc. However, the significance of Hurricane Katrina goes well beyond disaster assistance training or psychiatric syndromes. Hurricane Katrina is frequently referred to as the most devastating natural disaster in recent United States history. The storm was relentless in intensity and battered New Orleans and much of the Gulf region. Further, Hurricane Katrina came on the heels of the terrorist attacks on New York, Washington, D.C., and Pennsylvania. These events, separately, but especially when taken together, delivered a meaningful blow to U.S. Society and our psyche.

Hurricane Katrina and 9/11, after all, assaulted the leading civilization of its time. As with the Roman Empire, the Moor Kingdom, and other leading civilizations, the inhabitants feel much safer, even anointed, than those of concurrent nations. Succinctly, a feeling of invulnerability begins to pervade the common and individual consciousness. Hurricane Katrina and 9/11 struck at the heart of our sense of invulnerability. While 9/11 continually casts a shadow of apprehension as one awaits or attempts to prevent another occurrence, Hurricane Katrina is nature at work. Further, 9/11 is viewed by many as a failure of our government to protect us. Hurricane Katrina, however, hurts more—too many people. It speaks to our failure to care for ourselves; to care and protect our mothers, fathers, sisters, brothers, children, and neighbors.

Suffering such a blow, Hurricane Katrina demands that we reflect as a culture. One can see in that context that any analysis must extend beyond our "helper" role, our "techniques", or our "professional training". While these areas are vital to preparing ourselves to respond better in the future, the truer, more meaningful lessons are lost if that is largely the sum total of our analysis of the Katrina event. Simply put, to truly search for understanding the impact of Hurricane Katrina, one must dig deeper. We must burrow into ourselves, our society, issues of race, gender, class, and culture. Perhaps through such an exploration, a deeper understanding, or one that is closer to the deepest hurt that Katrina laid on all of us, may become more apparent and useful. It is, perhaps, the path to learning the true lessons and moving forward.

As with other cities, the Mayor of Philadelphia offered to shelter, care, and provide support for 1000 families affected by Katrina. The current paper recounts our role, as the organization selected by the Mayor, in welcoming and addressing the emotional impact of the storm on the evacuees. The goal is to explore the ethical and cultural issues, to contribute to, and keep alive, the quest for making sense of the event and improving society. The areas of interest are personal and professional. First, there will be a discussion of ethics in the context of working with Hurricane Katrina evacuees. Considering that the population was largely Black and poor, often a group considered voiceless, the responsible thing to do is to make ethics a central focus. Following that, the presentation becomes more personal and views the dynamics underlying Hurricane Katrina through the prisms of self awareness, our collective, personal, and racial identities, gender, economic class, and other ways one categorized humans. Lastly, we briefly touch on the fact that opportunity often accompanies tragedy, hope is always near, and explore some of those opportunities.

Ethics in the Eye of the Storm

Broadly speaking, as a mental health organization employing a range of professionals, one faces a consistent need to balance the codes of conduct with the needs of the evacuees and the desires of the city. While there were no requests for behavior that was blatant in violation of the code or with intent to harm, ethical issues are by nature sticky. Often, the attempt to service people quickly, fairly, and appropriately raised the specter of not fully embracing the strictest interpretations of the guidelines representing various codes.

The first ethical question faced was whether the code itself mattered since the evacuees were not patients or in a therapeutic relationship. Of course, we concluded that the code should still apply for the welfare and protection of the evacuees. Also, it is not good practice to begin such an endeavor by throwing out the code on the first day.

In any event, some of the difficulty existed simply because of the physical conditions of the site. So, for example, private rooms were not always available. However, one could balance this reality with the need for privacy and confidentiality that the evacuees, like anyone, should receive.

In the case of psychology, our area of practice, one is guided by Principles such as Beneficence and non-maleficence: benefit those with whom we work & take care to do no harm. Competence is also highlighted by the code. By the strictest standard, emergency or not, if one does not have specific training in disaster intervention then they should not have a role. However, our code is for psychologists. Prior to implementing the operation, here are several other dilemmas we discussed:

- What is the impact of our ethical code in the disaster setting?
- Do Emergency situations (providing service overrides not assisting) require flexibility with interpreting the code?
- How does one balance what one is legitimately and reasonably asked to do with one's code?
- Does the code only apply to therapeutic relationships that are clearly established?
- While not in the role of a psychologist, if you use your skill as a psychologist are you then bound by the code?
- What, if any, is the code for other mental health disciplines?; Are their codes less strict?
- Are unlicensed mental health professionals bound to any ethical code?

Thus, the above issues and others influenced how tasks/roles are delegated and the standards we set.

Who Do You Use?

Naturally, many people were motivated to assist Hurricane Katrina evacuees in Philadelphia. Our task, however, was to care for the evacuees emotionally. The task requires a skill level and sensitivity that outweighed the preparation level of most people wanting to help. Thus, we had to develop clear guidelines for who would assist and encourage others to find other venues for meeting their desire to help. The magnitude of the tragedy, and the desire for a united community, of course made it difficult to not accept any and all individuals attempting to be helpful. Various people were offering to help out.

First and foremost, the selection of individuals hinged on one's interpersonal and engagement skills. Simply put, one needed to be personable, respectful, warm, friendly, and inviting. Considering the fragility and chaos of the situation, any other interpersonal stance would likely be experienced as a betrayal by the evacuees.

You've Done This Before Right?

A second criterion we set included determining whether the person is qualified to provide clinical services, despite the ambiguity of our charge. We determined that it was important that the helpful have a more precise ability to ascertain whether more intensive behavioral health services were needed by the evacuee. A second criterion included assessing whether the interested helper had experience in disaster and/or complicated emotional situations. Experience with certain populations, for example families and substance use, were given priority.

You're Not Here To Get Over On These Folks, Right?

A third factor that ranked high in making judgments about appropriateness of the task was knowledge of and commitment to ethical conduct. The reality is that many of the evacuees are from backgrounds where they may not advocate for themselves or are at risk for being exploited by someone with perceived power.

So, various ethical considerations became evident during the engagement process, primarily focused around conflicts between traditional psychotherapy, crisis intervention and disaster intervention. It rapidly became clear that the typical means of engagement were not valid here. For example, the designated mental health area was inviting under the false assumption that the various guests would be more seeking of support. Quickly, however, one learns that one is more successful engaging individuals in walks to the bathroom or to the cafeteria.

With the aim of balancing the code and the reality, we came to several conclusions. Overall, it is important during crises to prioritize ethical issues and determine strategies for their management. In addition, the prioritizing includes having a template to determine the appropriateness of boundary crossing during natural disasters. As important, keep in sight the intent of the code: the Welfare & protection of individuals/groups with whom we work.

Specifically, we found the following conclusions immeasurably helpful as a framework for preparing staff and effectively servicing the evacuees while adhering to the code:

- Balance the demands of the code with the reality of the situation: (Consider how is one's code relevant in this setting?)
- Precisely understand what your goal is with others (Define what you are actually doing with people….putting the patient/guest first.)
- Focus on helping the person and not the code (Where does your allegiance lie, adhering to the code or helping someone?)
- The Code is not the end itself, it's a means to an end (Don't ignore the code, but there is a different focus)

Culture and Engagement in the Eye of the Storm

Unifying event

In many ways the events surrounding Hurricane Katrina have undoubtedly served a positive role in our society. It has seemingly removed the rose-colored glasses that we have needed in an attempt to avoid racial tensions and avoid the belief that we are still largely relationally influenced by race. We, as Americans, fancy ourselves to exist as a "melting-pot" society with immeasurable cognitive flexibility regarding issues of cultural diversity. We tell ourselves, of course we should be beyond this. We believe ourselves to have learned from our past experiences of race conflict in the US and to have embraced a remarkably culturally tolerant means of functioning. Hurricane Katrina has served as somewhat of a unifying event, as we collectively experience a flooding of consciousness, of what race means in our relational world. We become stripped of our defensive denial and confronted with the reality of our 2005 racial world. As blacks we are left to mourn the loss of the delusion of equal footing, and confront the associated anger and frustration. In the case of our white counterparts there is a loss of their ability to maintain their denial and blindness to the influence of race in our world.

Evacuee presentation

The evacuees of New Orleans faced many challenges prior to Hurricane Katrina. The residents present as a group that, based on large indicators, struggles as a community. The following is a summary of New Orleans residents. Part 1 is demographic and part 2 is impressions upon meeting the evacuees in Philadelphia.

The evacuees in New Orleans were overwhelmingly Black. For the population of New Orleans, 69 % are Black or African American; 28 % White. Economically, in 2004, 23 percent of people in New Orleans were in poverty. Further, 14% of all families and 29 % of families with a female householder and no husband present had incomes below the poverty level. Finally, over half of the population in New Orleans rents housing. Lastly unemployment estimates range from 11.8 to 13.8%. (Source: U.S. Census Bureau, 2004 American Community Survey)

Meeting the Evacuees

The presentation of the survivors themselves included everything from denial, numbness, detachment, disorientation, anger, and depression. One is struck by what seemed to be a sense of loss, most notably a loss in the ability to trust, undoubtedly further compounded by the seemingly competitive climate of volunteers during the first few days at Wanamaker. For many, Hurricane Katrina seemed to exacerbate pre-existing issues of distrust of society and themselves in relation to it. Having resided within the impoverished environment of New Orleans, and the significant influence of access to scarce resources and residing within chaotic/aggressive neighborhoods, prior to Katrina, many of the evacuees manifested an untrusting and aggressive relational style.

Their unique racial/cultural perceptive seemed to play a significant role in their response to the disaster, notably provoking their underlying lack of trust in outside entities. The intense emotions invoked by the trauma were frequently channeled into vilification of the government in its entirety and anyone perceived to be related to that system. Subsequently, there was distinct resistance towards many of the people who provided assistance in the aftermath based on an underlying and now heightened sense of distrust. The exacerbation of this pre-existing distrust was further manifested through extensive conspiracy theories and a hostile sense of entitlement towards the government.

Their anger and paranoia was fully valid, as they harshly and painfully confronted their own vulnerability. Forced, based on a natural disaster, to confront their true dependence on a society that in the light of day they believed showed them that they were seemingly disposable. Conspiracy theories were rampant. There was clear questioning by the evacuees of why you were there, why were you interested in supposedly "helping" them. Everyone's motives were clearly in question.

This resistance also induced several reactions in those that sought to assist in their recovery, calling for an awareness of the unique cultural issues that exist with many lower income African Americans, specifically as it relates to their subsequent relational style. Staff bared the responsibility of not personalizing the expressions of anger and distrust but being comfortable with not avoiding their genuine expression of pain and hurt, often presented in an uncensored and raw form. The task became to become sensitive to their individual concerns and issues, in a manner that truly met them where they were in their experience instead of forcing them into traditional formal psychotherapy.

Several guests were indeed desperate to gain attention and validation of their anger, demanding respect and understanding of their experience. They were desperate to establish some small measure of control in the midst of an event that in almost every way thus far they had been unable to gain any control. Whether it was their lack of control regarding resources to evacuate to a safe location other than the Louisiana Superdome before the hurricane, lack of control in how they were treated while residing in the Superdome, lack of control following the failure of the levees and lack of control in being able to escape the ill infants, dead bodies, or life threatening conditions they were forced to endure, unable to control for the safety of their children, their wives their husbands, or unable to control where they were evacuated to, all were affected. Many of the evacuees reported boarding a flight and being informed that they were headed for Texas but were instead brought to Philadelphia, under duress, by armed sky marshals.

Confronted with Reality

Although I cannot notably recall my initial experience of hearing the radio news I undoubtedly recall the circumstances surrounding my experience of the first visual images of the Superdome. I clearly remember my experience of coming home from work to relax on the couch and turning on the evening news to see countless images of black suffering. As a young black woman, my generation had been far removed from any notable experience of racial tensions, hearing only historical accounts from one's elders or through historical documentaries. The realness of the events was undeniably shocking. Was it possible to actually be viewing such images in 2005? Surely we as a society were not capable of having such human tragedy with such a delayed response.

In viewing images of the Superdome following the Hurricane and subsequent dam failure, issues of one's true vulnerability as an African American within our society is provoked. One is no longer able to maintain the belief and psychological denial that race is not as salient of an issue in our society as in eras past. Nor is one able to deny the anger associated with this reality. One becomes unable to maintain the self-delusion that has played such a pivotal role in assisting in one's ability to succeed in the world, and one becomes faced with a decisive challenge of sorts. Indeed there exists a pivotal juncture that arguably all blacks must face - to embrace the inescapable stereotypes associated with being an African American within our society and either allowing those stereotypes to strangle one's self-motivation and belief in one's ability to succeed despite them or gain perspective and integrate them in some meaningful way as fuel to drive one's ambitions. Of course, this decision is not always conscious and may unconsciously influence us on several levels. At some point, all blacks, to some degree, must confront the fear of embracing the reality of the situation, a situation that can easily paralyze one against action. Of course, the multigenerational beliefs of one's immediate family and additional outside supports greatly mediate one's concept of self, self in relation to the outside world, and subsequently our consolidation of a racial identity. Reconciling this issue, however, becomes required to function, to believe that achievement and success is possible in the face of such obstacles. If resolved in favor of achievement, one must additionally address the reality of what it means to leave behind other fellow blacks whom have been unable to escape the stereotypes that handicap them from achieving. In our quest to succeed, this conflict can contribute to the desire to distance ourselves from non-achievement oriented blacks, distinguish ourselves from our more unsuccessful counterparts, and in distinguishing ourselves, move away from and shatter the negative stereotypes regarding our blackness. Or do we? In facing the images of Hurricane Katrina and the Superdome one cannot distance oneself from the suffering faces of individuals that undoubtedly share a similar skin color and similar facial features, individuals whose suffering we are now confronted with on every television channel. Our wounds become exposed, wounds inflicted from our experiences of race in our society. Through various means we have tried to mask such narcissistic injuries, attempting to deny them into nonexistence in favor of achievement. However, now one is inescapably faced with our racial vulnerability.

The Influence of racial identity

In my inner psychic world, there is the reality that as a successful black woman I am guilty of having basked in my feeling of being separate from such uneducated and poverty stricken individuals, that happen to share the same race as I. Yet I am now confronted with the inescapable emotional pain inflicted by watching events unfold in the Superdome and recognizing my own vulnerability. I am left with the feeling that once I leave my home, I will walk in the world with my injuries exposed.

Following the bombardment of television images I look forward to arriving to work, to my African American counterparts. longing to have my anger and frustration validated by those I know will understand. I cannot recall the exact time frame from when I entered the doors of my office to my first attempt to facilitate a discussion and feel calmed by those who without me saying a single word I know I will feel connection. People who are also today struggling with who they are in relation to their society, a world that we all have felt has improved significantly, that we all have needed to feel has improved significantly to function and achieve. But yet we are faced with a changed climate.

I attentively listen to the radio to hear current thoughts and opinions, listening for vocal tones that hint at the race of the individual speaking, curious of the non-black perspective, curious if they feel even a ripple of what I feel as a black woman whom now exists somehow changed, hypersensitive to my racial environment.

Volunteering

Many of these issues are what directly contribute to a personal desire to volunteer. Volunteering to minimize feelings of helplessness and concentrate one's thoughts and energies towards positive meaningful interaction/intervention. *To use my inner resources to stave off immobility and disequilibrium.* Although, one cannot claim to have known each individual person's personal motivations, some patterns of intentions seemed evident. There were:

Blacks whom seemed to perceive their volunteering as a:

- A chance to make amends and identify with members they have distanced themselves from.
- A chance to meaningfully contribute and give back to their community

Whites whom:

- confront feelings of guilt as members of white society with its associated privileges seemed to be operating under a belief that they have not contributed enough
- were in a state of bargaining, that if they were to make this contribution that the reality of our world would be disproved

And those across races:

- whom seemingly sought to be in the middle of it all, to be able to say that they were there
- whom assumed the role of bearing witness to the tragedy, so it is kept alive in our consciousness

Of course, the therapist gain cannot be ignored; selfishly there is the professional desire to be affiliated with the recovery efforts allowing our professional egos to be stroked. Evacuee perception of this gain was also evident as individuals, eager to be associated with them, often swarmed them.

In the search of probing one's self with the aim of uncovering important drivers of one's actions and behaviors, we came to several conclusions. In particular, we found the following useful for conceptualizing the many influences, including racial identity, that impact performance:

- The importance of self-analysis in the management of intense emotional responses evoked in assisting survivors of a natural disaster
- That recognizing racial and cultural factors is not enough to meet our responsibilities as helpers.
- The necessity of integrating issues of racial identity and culture into a dynamic understanding of survivors and their treatment needs

Making Sense of it all

Overall, the experience of Hurricane Katrina has served a marked role in our society, it has forced us to reevaluate our racial beliefs, challenge our sense of social responsibility, and put our own humanity into perspective. It has demanded that we recognize the most fragile members of our society and acknowledge our sense of responsibility to ourselves. Not only does it become our task to develop racial and cultural treatment protocols but also to challenge what it means to truly respect them as contributing members of our society.

We also cannot ignore the significance of this event as an opportunity to gain increased perspective regarding both the positive changes in our society and the negative influences that continue to permeate our relationships and actions, in addition to, gain perspective regarding one's own social responsibility. By owning the reality of this event and its implications regarding our racial society, putting the loss of our delusions into perspective, and recognizing the potential for societal growth, it can then serve a motivational impetus. Impetus to make a self-assessment of what one's individual role as a member of our society is to improve race relations and determine how we can use our unique strengths and discover potential rather than limits.

References

Brown, A., (2005) <u>Hurricane Katrina Pummels Three States</u> (Transcript of CNN Newsnight with Aaron Brown). Department of Homeland security (DHS.com)

Fagot, Winbush, D., (2006) <u>Hurricane Katrina/Hurricane Rita Evacuation and Production Shut-in Statistics Report as of Wednesday, February 22.</u> U.S. Government Minerals Management Service.

Knabb, R; Rhome, J.; Brown, D., (2005) <u>Tropical Cyclone Report: Hurricane Katrina</u>: 23-30 August 2005. National Hurricane Center.

Krupa, M (2006).<u>Presumed Missing.</u> Times-Picayune.

Louisiana Department of Health and Hospitals (2006) <u>Reports of Missing and Deceased</u>.

Phillips, K., (2005) <u>Bush Discusses Displaced Students; Department of Defense Briefs Press on Katrina Response</u> (CNN Live Transcript).

Sheikh, P., (2005) <u>The Impact of Hurricane Katrina on Biological Resources</u> (PDF). Congressional Research Service.

Staff Writer, (2005) "The Aftermath of Katrina" Transcript of CNN Live Saturday. CNN.

Staff writer., (2005) "Hurricane Katrina Situation Report No. 3." Florida State Emergency.

Staff Writer, (2006) "Deaths of evacuees push toll to 1,577". New Orleans Times-Picayune.

Staff Writer., (2006) "Katrina Heads for New Orleans." Fox News/Associated Press. August 29, 2005.

U.S. Census Bureau, (2004) <u>American Community Survey</u>

United States Department of Commerce (2006) <u>Hurricane Katrina Service Assessment Report</u>

About the Authors

Kenneth Glass, Ph.D. is a licensed Psychologist who specializes in public health issues (e.g. violence, trauma), treatment in the inner city, clinical and cultural engagement, racial identity, organizational development, and resilience. Dr. Glass received his Ph.D. in clinical psychology from Columbia University and has a Finance Certificate from Harvard Business School. He is the Chief Executive Officer at WES Health System, the largest African American-managed behavioral health organization in Pennsylvania. He has extensive clinical and administrative experience in community mental health in Philadelphia, New York City, and Boston. African

American Psychology has two major schools of thought, Nigresence and Africentrist, and Dr. Glass had the singular fortune of training under the pre-eminent scholar of each viewpoint, Drs. Robert T. Carter and Hussein A. Bulhan, respectively. Dr. Glass' dissertation is the only integration of the two theoretical approaches. Dr. Glass was a program committee member for 5 years at The Roundtable at Columbia University, the nation's largest and longest running conference devoted to cultural issues in treatment. The City of Boston went more than 19 months in 1995-1996 without a child under the age of 18 dying as a result of violence. In 1985, Dr. Glass was an establishing member of the lead agency for the City of Boston's effort, which functioned under the direction of the Dr. Deborah Prothrow-Stith, a nation figure on youth violence and Dean at the Harvard School of Public Health.

Tasha Elizabeth Graves, M.S. is an advanced year Clinical Psychology Doctoral Student at Chestnut Hill College. She received her Master's in Counseling Psychology with a Specialization in Child and Adolescent Therapy from Chestnut Hill College and Bachelors in Psychology from Bloomsburg University. She is currently affiliated with WES Health System as a clinical consultant and previous Director of Family Based Services, out of which she provided services to evacuees of Hurricane Katrina. She has been providing clinical services to a variety of clientele for over 9 years providing individual and family therapy, consultation services, clinical supervision, and crisis management. Ms. Graves has additionally served as a trainer and consultant with several Philadelphia based treatment organizations with specific focus in case conceptualization, treatment planning, crisis intervention, Posttraumatic Stress Disorder, and suicide prevention. Her clinical skills have been recognized with invitations to present at several national conferences. The diversity of her experiences have included residential, outpatient, and community based services.

Research interests and pursuits include object relations oriented psychotherapy, treatment of trauma, and working with urban populations. Affiliations include the American Psychological Association, and the Pennsylvania Psychological Association.

Resolving Distress: The Medical Myth
By John Durkin

Abstract

The medical-model as it applies to psychological trauma and its resolution follows that of addressing physical trauma in that it requires a set of symptoms to generate a diagnosis that proposes a specific course of treatment. The argument that the medical-model may not be appropriate to the resolution of psychological trauma was made by the humanistic psychology movement and has been made more recently in positive psychology. Pointing out that the medical-model ignores the positive aspects of adversity, positive psychologists argue for a viewpoint that acknowledges a greater range of human experience than is possible through a focus on exclusively negative symptoms. In recognition of the positive as well as the negative consequences of traumatic experience, a brief, practical and clinically-relevant measure of well-being that can be used in the post-traumatic aftermath will be introduced.

John Durkin is a psychologist specializing in stress-resolution and post-traumatic growth. He is an accredited trainer in critical incident stress management and working toward his PhD at the University of Nottingham, UK

Growth through Adversity

Positive psychological changes in the aftermath of distressing and difficult experiences have been recognized and discussed in many fields of human endeavor including literature, philosophy and religion (Tedeschi, Park & Calhoun, 1998). Empirical studies have been undertaken that have also demonstrated enhanced psychological health amongst those suffering a range of serious acute and chronic medical challenges including cancer, heart attack and addiction. One term that has been given to this benign adaptation to threatening events is "adversarial growth" (Linley & Joseph, 2004). Clinicians have been urged to take account of the possibility of positive change in the aftermath of traumatic experience and were reminded that post-traumatic stress disorder interventions rarely acknowledge adversarial growth even though it has been shown to be related to lower distress (Linley and Joseph, 2004).

Positive Psychology

Positive psychology is a movement that takes the perspective of humanistic psychology as its foundation (Seligman, Steen, Park and Peterson, 2005) and has been built largely in line with the movement led by Rogers and Maslow in the 1950's and '60s (Joseph & Linley, 2006). The humanistic movement in its client- (or person-centered) view, and latterly the positive psychology movement, acknowledged the range of human experience in the resolution of psychological distress and its reliance on the assumption of an innate tendency towards growth. This compares with the medical-model focus of categorizing distress and offering treatment for negative symptoms to the exclusion of any positive consequences, such as growth, following adversity. This bias towards the negative features of traumatic experience has drawn criticism from some positive psychologists who argue against the "medicalization" of such experience (e.g. Maddux, Snyder & Lopez, 2004). The medical-model viewpoint is seemingly an influential one given its appearance in some authoritative guidance on treatment for post-traumatic stress disorder (PTSD).

Treatment Guidelines for Post–Traumatic Stress Disorder

In March 2005, the National Institute for Clinical Excellence (NICE) issued guidelines to the National Health Service in the United Kingdom (UK) on the treatment of PTSD. Treatment recommendations were restricted to trauma-focused cognitive-behavioural therapy (TF-CBT), eye-movement desensitization and reprocessing (EMDR) and drug therapies where TF-CBT or EMDR proved unsuccessful.

Early in the guidelines, the authors offer the following advice:

> Initial response to trauma:
> • For individuals who have experienced a traumatic event, the systematic provision to that individual alone of brief, single-session interventions (often referred to as debriefing) that focus on the traumatic incident, should not be routine practice when delivering services.
> • Where symptoms are mild and have been present for less than 4 weeks after the trauma, watchful waiting, as a way of managing the difficulties presented by people with post-traumatic stress disorder (PTSD), should be considered. A follow-up contact should be arranged within 1 month. (Gaskell & The British Psychological Society, 2005)

The first point warns against the use of an intervention called "debriefing" although no definition of debriefing was given in the guidelines. Reference was made however, to a Cochrane Review (e.g. Rose, Bisson, Churchill & Wessely, 2002) that investigated psychological debriefing in preventing post-traumatic stress disorder and which reported two studies; one study that showed no benefit and one that suggested the prospect of harm, both in studies on hospital patients. Critical Incident Stress Debriefing (CISD: Mitchell, 1983), the structured group-based intervention initially developed for emergency personnel, was cited, adapted and used in those studies. To those familiar with the "Mitchell-model" the idea of a return to function is a stated aim of the intervention and one which, if the focus of a psychological investigation is to be thoroughly assessed, should be measured. While a positive-model view might anticipate such progress, the medical-model view may overlook restored function, especially where negative symptoms persisted.

The second point recommends "watchful waiting" for up to four weeks after a traumatic incident of those who present with symptoms. Waiting one month for a follow-up (another unspecified procedure) was not explained but does coincide with the duration criterion between event and PTSD that would justify a diagnosis according to the DSM-IV (American Psychological Association, 1994). In practice it would appear that beyond the observation of emergent symptoms during the post-incident period, no intervention is recommended.

Crisis Intervention

The practice of crisis intervention has been described and reported since the First World War when the principles of "Immediacy, Proximity and Expectancy" were advanced to promote the idea of acting quickly to restore normality in soldiers following combat. These principles were built on in the development of CISM but which also advocated peer-support as the psychosocial medium through which crisis-intervention should be undertaken. Crisis-intervention can be seen as a person-centered approach as it presumes little expertise on the part of the interventionist for knowledge of the other's condition, but seeks to provide the safe environment necessary for the affected individual to express themselves authentically. The cognitive and emotional elements of the experience can be linked in a supportive environment to generate the meaning that leads to a new understanding and growth.

Traumatic Incident Reduction

Traumatic Incident Reduction (TIR: Gerbode, 1995) is a structured, theoretically driven, person-centered approach for resolution with highly distressed individuals, a model aligned with principles described by Rogers (1959; Joseph & Worsley, 2005). Whereas the medicalization of traumatic stress has led to the perception that helping people overcome the effects of adverse experiences requires highly trained and expensive expert intervention, proponents of the TIR approach argue that distress following adverse experiences is indicative of normal processes of recovery, and that these processes can be facilitated by non-expert peer-support.

The medical model, as in the example of the NICE guidelines discussed above, offers access to treatment following diagnosis. It was noted however, that problematic symptoms have to emerge in order to justify a diagnosis as only "watchful waiting" was advised for up to four weeks before referral. Depending on the resources available for treatment an indefinite wait could ensue, even where treatment was urgent. Offering a treatment regimen based entirely on the negative consequences of a distressing event is likely to paint an incomplete picture of the experience of the individual. To present a diagnosis, in the view of those who employ person-centered practices such as crisis-intervention and TIR, is to medicalize a normal recovery process. It is foreseeable that to diagnose and so describe the early stages of recovery as a mental illness, with the associated stigma, could undermine the efforts of some to overcome their current problems. Alternatively, seeing distress on a continuum of functioning, rather than as the presence or absence of negative symptoms, would at least acknowledge the presence of positive elements in the recovery process that would be ignored in the medical view.

Assessing Well-Being

In addition, the notion of a continuum of functioning with negative aspects at one end and positive aspects at the other would enable, with appropriate measurement, the recognition of movement along that continuum as a means to monitoring recovery. Such a continuum, and a simple measurement tool, has been described in the development of the Short Depression Happiness Scale (SDHS: Joseph, Linley, Harwood, Lewis & McCollam (2004). The SDHS correlates well with both the Beck Depression Inventory (Beck & Steer, 1987) and the Oxford Happiness Inventory (Argyle, Martin, & Crossland, 1989). The scale uses six statements with a 0-3 response scale for each statement giving a 0-18 scoring range. Low scores on the SDHS correlate with depressive symptoms while higher scores represent increasing happiness. This brief measure allows for the rapid measurement of overall psychological well-being. Repeated measurements would identify movement along the continuum in a positive direction to indicate recovery, or in a negative direction to identify ongoing difficulties.

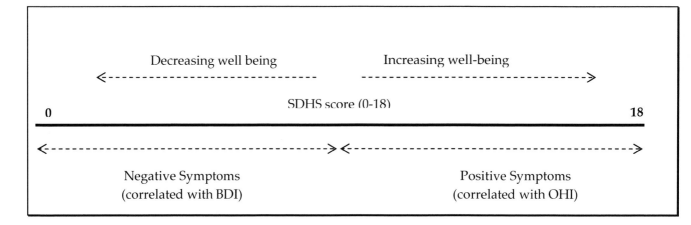

Figure 1. Continuum of functioning measured by Short Depression Happiness Scale (Joseph et al., 2004)

Conclusion

The alternative paradigm to the medical model that was described by the early humanistic psychologists can find support for its claims by employing such a brief assessment at different stages of a post-traumatic aftermath. Not only is there measurement of a greater range of emotional expression, but also evidence can be accrued for the defining assumption that individuals are intrinsically motivated towards growth and fulfillment. A number of crisis-intervention, clinical treatment or social-environmental factors can be employed and their effects measured quickly and effectively using the SDHS.

Practitioners of TIR (see <www.tir.org> have begun to employ the SDHS formally in order to give weight to their success with their person-centered model and to generate empirical evidence of change following sessions. While evaluations of success within the medical-model are bound by the limitations of measuring the reduction of negative symptoms, they necessarily overlook important features of recovery that are beneficial and fulfilling such as coming to terms with the setback of an adverse life-event. With the influence of the medical-model on clinical guidance for resolving traumatic stress, it would appear that the development of innovative and novel approaches will be constrained. With the SDHS there is a simple and brief measure that can be applied in numerous post-trauma settings to help establish both reduction in negative symptoms and positive improvements in well-being. The use of the SDHS with a group of practitioners working in a structured, person-centered model and measuring their effects with a brief and clinically relevant assessment tool represents an interesting and challenging alternative to the medical viewpoint of stress-resolution.

About the Author

John Durkin, Msc is a psychologist specializing in the stress of fire, rescue and emergency work. As a firefighter he was medically retired with PTSD and upon graduation became accredited as a Trainer of Critical Incident Stress Management (CISM) with the International

Critical Incident Stress Foundation (ICISF). He is Chair of the Research Committee of the Traumatic Incident Reduction Association (TIRA) and sits on the Board of Applied Metapsychology International (AMI). John is embarking on a PhD at the University of Nottingham with a research program investigating a person-centered approach to the resolution of distress in occupations at high-risk for PTSD.

References

American Psychiatric Association (1994) *Diagnostic and statistical manual of mental disorders* (4th Ed) Washington, DC: Author.

Argyle, M., Martin, M., & Crossland, J. (1989) Happiness as a function of personality and social encounters. In J. P. Forgas & J. M. Innes (Eds.), *Recent advances in social psychology: An international perspective*. North Holland: Elsevier.

Beck, A.T. & Steer, R.A. (1987) *Beck Depression Inventory Manual*. San Antonio, TX: The Psychological Corporation.

Gaskell & The British Psychological Society (2005) Post-traumatic Stress Disorder: The management of PTSD in adults and children in primary and secondary care. National Clinical Practice Guideline Number 26.

Gerbode, F.A. (1995) Beyond Psychology: An Introduction to Metapsychology. 3rd edn. IRM Press, California.

Joseph, S., & Linley, P. A. (2006). Positive psychology versus the medical model. American Psychologist, 61 , 332-333.

Joseph, S., & Worsley, R. (2005). Person-centered psychopathology: A positive psychology of mental health. PCCS books: Ross-on-Wye

Joseph, S., Linley, P. A., Harwood, J., Lewis, C. A., & McCollam, P. (2004). Rapid assessment of well-being: The Short Depression-Happiness Scale (SDHS). *Psychology and Psychotherapy: Theory, Research and Practice, 77,* 1-14.

Maddux, J.E., Snyder, C.R. & Lopez S.J. (2004) Toward a positive clinical psychology: Deconstructing the illness ideology and constructing an ideology of human strengths and potential. In P.A. Lindley & S. Joseph

Mitchell, J. T. (1983) When disaster strikes…the critical incident stress debriefing process. Journal of Emergency Medical Services; 8:36–39

Rose S, Bisson J, Churchill R, Wessely S. Psychological debriefing for preventing post traumatic stress disorder (PTSD). Cochrane Database of Systematic Reviews: Reviews 2002 Issue 2 John Wiley & Sons, Ltd Chichester, UK

Seligman, M.E.P., Steen, T.A., Park, N. & Peterson, C. (2005) Positive psychology progress: Empirical validation of interventions. *American Psychologist, 60,* 410-421.

Tedeschi, R.G, Park, C.L. and Calhoun, L.G. (eds) (1998) *Posttraumatic Growth changes in the aftermath of crisis.* Mahway: Lawrence Erlbaum.

The Dissociation of Abigail:
A Psychodynamic and Behavioral Assessment

Alan L. Hensley, PhD Candidate, BCETS, FAAETS

Capella University
Minneapolis, Minnesota

Abstract

Among the most profound manifestations of childhood trauma is that of Dissociative Identity Disorder (DID). Theorists suggest DID can be both adaptive and dysfunctional in nature. The Dissociation of Abigail will illustrate how childhood trauma can affect the perception, cognition, and behavior of an individual into their adult years. This case study will discuss client intake, assessment, and potential treatment.

Abigail, a tall, attractive, and well-groomed divorced mother of 5 children in her late 30s, presents herself in the therapist's office complaining of the inability to remember key periods of her life. Discussion with the client reveals she is, in fact, extremely intelligent, intuitive, and well versed on a myriad of subjects; including an acute knowledge of psychology that would arguably be the envy of many professional therapists. Within moments of beginning the intake, the therapist becomes keenly aware that this client is also exceedingly spiritual, with the ability to quote chapter and verse of biblical reference, not only as a matter of reference, but with the insight to integrate it in context with a myriad of contemporary issues.

As the therapist listens, Abigail recounts a lifetime of sexual abuse and boundary violations by family members of not only herself, but also two of her children. The client complains of an inability to recall diverse periods of her life. Recently, however, she has begun experiencing recurring psychologically and emotionally distressing, thoughts, images, and dreams of satanic rituals involving family members and persons and places of her childhood in which she is forced to participate. The client offers her life has been accentuated with dysfunctional relationships. Consequently, she is prone to reclusion, and has little interest in outside persons, places, or activities, which significantly impairs social, occupational, and other activities.

Predisposed to consider Abigail's symptoms in context of *Posttraumatic Stress Disorder* (PTSD) (American Psychiatric Association, 2000), the therapist is presented with two lengthy journals Abigail has maintained at the request of her current therapist. Within the first journal, disjointed transitions are noted, alternating between first, second, and third person, present- and past-tense. While the journal opens with eloquence and exceptionally light-handed penmanship and flourishes, it unexpectedly transitions to heavy-handedness with angry intonations directed at Abigail herself. As the journey through the journals continues, several other such transitions are noted, along with highly distinctive differences in penmanship and writing style.

More importantly, the writings reflect distinct differences in cognitive process. Cryptanalysis of the writings discloses six psychologically significant profiles, as if six different individuals were writing the journals. Disjointed and appearing unexpectedly independent junctures, they appeared to be conflicted and often vying for dominance in expressing their opinions and beliefs. If one were to thematically categorize these six profiles into individual context, they would find *the intellectual* (strives for intellect and perfection); *the preacher* (core of morals, ethics, and values); *the abuser* (the mother); *the victim* (childlike; timid, shy, and afraid); *the reckoner* (endeavors to evoke shame and deliver punishment); and a highly pronounced highly sexual *vixen* personality (sexually motivated, arguably the personality for male gratification/survival).

Client History

Assessment and therapeutic intervention of Abigail's complaints are seen to be problematic without examining current perception, cognition, and behavior in context with her abusive past. During intake, Abigail reveals several salient factors that must be considered during assessment. The childhood family infrastructure is described as dysfunctional, with Abigail and her father in opposition to her mother and her bothers. The client describes an environment of social deprivation, in which she repeatedly characterizes her family as fundamental cultists and survivalists. Abigail's assertions are supported in a family biography authored by her mother, in which her family relocated to increasingly reclusive environments in Washington and remote Alaska. The client suggests the family relocated to remote Alaska following the death (suspected suicide) of her older brother. Writings by the client's mother include a harrowing life-threatening incident involving Abigail and her brother, as well as the death and dismemberment of her pet dog by a wolf.

Factual or fictional, Abigail recalls intense ritualistic victimization by family and others during her childhood. The client now suggests recurring sexual molestation by her father, mother, and other family members, often during such ritualistic circumstances.

Education was achieved largely through correspondence courses, which again, has been confirmed in family writings. Consequently, the client was deprived of extra-family socialization and peer interaction during her formative years. However, Abigail's final two years of high school were completed in a nearby town in Alaska, during which the she did not reside with her family. Following graduation, Abigail returned to Washington, while her family remained in Alaska. Abigail's parents divorced shortly after her graduation and departure from Alaska.

Abigail reveals a pattern of dysfunctional relationships during adulthood, including her marriage to a man she describes as being both controlling and manipulative. As the therapist listens, Abigail describes a marriage devoid of mutual satisfaction and attentiveness. Instead, she describes a marriage in which she is unable to establish and maintain equity or boundaries until her son revealed that his father was sexually molesting both him and his sister. Her then husband argued that it was the son who was abusing his sister. Consequently, the son was removed from the family home. Subsequent events and investigation, however, revealed it was, in fact, Abigail's former husband committing the egregious behavior. Abigail and her children separated from him and a divorce was subsequently granted.

Perhaps more troubling was the disclosure that during a visit prior to the separation, Abigail's mother too was sexually abusing her grandchildren. With her father deceased, Abigail estranged herself from her mother. As Abigail's marriage failed, she and her five children were without a support system during a period when they needed one most.

Following her divorce, Abigail discloses a pattern of promiscuity; frequently confusing the physical act of sex with love, including a sexual interlude with her male counselor. Resultantly, her sexually motivated behavior, in direct opposition to her religious morals, ethics, and values, resulted in acute cognitive dissonance. As a result, Abigail avoids all situations in which such behavior is likely to occur.

Diagnostic Assessment

Axis I: Dissociative Disorder NOS (300.15)
> Posttraumatic Stress Disorder (309.81)
> Major Depressive Disorder, Recurrent, Severe W/O Psychotic Features (296.33)

Axis II: Relational Problems (V61.20 Parent-child; V61.1 Partner; V61.8 Siblings)

Axis III: None

AxisIV: Problems with primary support group and social environment; inability to obtain/maintain employment;

Axis V: GAF (Current) = 31
> GAF (Highest in Past Year) = 45

Literature Review

PTSD is a recognized mental disorder (309.81) catalogued in the Diagnostic and Statistical Manual of Mental Disorders, Fourth Edition, Text Revision (DSM-IV-TR; American Psychiatric Association, 2000). Unfortunately, the breadth of the effects of posttraumatic stress does not lend itself well to the restrictive boundaries afforded by the DSM-IV. Rather, the manifestation presents itself well beyond merely the psychological domain. In fact, the symptomology of PTSD might manifest in the biological or physical, psychological, and the sociological realms as well (van der Kolk, McFarlane, & Weisaeth, 1996; Scaer, 2001, 2005).

The *Bio-Psycho-Social Model* (Engel, 1977, 1980) lends itself well as the essential theoretical framework for assessment of persons afflicted with PTSD and comorbid disorders. The key feature of the Bio-Psycho-Social Model is the concept of holism. In essence, Engel (1977, 1980) suggests PTSD manifestation is precipitated by a clear external precipitating occurrence or event, which overwhelms our coping processes. The coping mechanisms are facilitated or mediated through the central nervous system, particularly the autonomic nervous system; and the HPA axis, which refers to the hypothalamus and the pituitary and adrenal glands of the brain. Thus, the bio-psycho-social model provides the essential framework for understanding the biological, psychological, and sociological aspects of PTSD and comorbid DID symptomology.

Theorists, such as van der Kolk et al. (1996) and Scaer (2001, 2005) offer that PTSD results from a complex interplay between the different parts of the brain that regulate both healthy and pathological thoughts, memories, feelings, and responses or behaviors. Among the extreme pathological responses is DID. Van der Kolk (1996), Scaer (2001, 2005), as well as the DSM-IV-TR (American Psychiatric Association, 2000) offer that intrusive dreams, persistent avoidance, inability to recall important aspects of the traumatic event(s), hypervigilance, and exaggerated startle response are symptomatic of PTSD. Perhaps, these symptoms embody the innate human desire for survival; the human mind in reaction to an incomprehensible event that threatens one's survival.

Likewise, Haddock (2001) suggests DID is about survival; a defensive mechanism that can be adaptive and dysfunctional at the same time. Haddock (2001) and Scaer (2001) both suggest, as a defensive measure, the mind encapsulates the traumatic experience, removing it from consciousness to prevent further biological, psychological, and physiological harm. As one is distanced from the trauma, the once adaptive and life-affirming defense becomes dysfunctional. The maladaptive responses are frequently beyond one's control; occur at inopportune times and places; and are often disruptive to his or her way of life. While DID is then adaptive in the sense that it helps insulate one from pain, it is also maladaptive in the present context as the individual begins to distort time, or might lose time and recall of experiences during the dissociative period altogether (Haddock, 2001).

Theoretical Basis for Dissociation

Hierarchy of needs

Fundamental to human perception, cognition, and behavior, Maslow (1970) proposes a hierarchy consisting of five levels of needs by which one navigates life's experiences—*physiological, safety, love/belonging, esteem,* and *self-actualization.* Subsequent theorists, discontented with such broad generalizations, added two levels. The revised hierarchy now depicts *physiological, security, love/belonging, validation, order/structure, aesthetics,* and *actualization.*

Maslow (1970) argued, in order to progress to each successive level, one must satisfy to underlying levels. While many might mistakenly believe that, once achieved, the levels are perpetually satisfied, Maslow (1970) suggests that the process is, in fact, highly dynamic. While one possesses the capability to strive for the next level, an equal possibility exist that, based upon life events, one might equally as well, descend to a previously satisfied level. In fact, one might ascend and descend the levels of need several times during their lifetime depending upon new experiences. Additionally, satisfaction of each level reflects not only the individual's perception, but also the factors contributing to one's perception of reality, including family, peers, sociocultural groups, and other environmental factors (Pervin, Cervone & Johns, 2005). Of relevance to the present case, one must consider the individual's placement in the hierarchy of needs to understand the significance of their perception, cognition, and behavior. For example, one might find it unnecessary to be concerned with aesthetics or order, when his or her physiological or safety needs are not being met.

Perry (2002) suggests while each child has unique genetic potential, studies point to important needs of every child, and long-term consequences for brain function if those needs are not met. Perry (2002), among others (Bremner, Southwick, & Charney, 1991), suggests experience, not only traumatic experience, directly influences not only future perception, cognition, and behavior, but biologically influences the victim's memory and personality as well. Consequently, assessment of one's personality and locus of control provides an indication of the presence and quality of traits and coping mechanisms that will be used to interact with future experiences. In the present proposed study, predisposition must be considered and assessed on an individual basis.

Stages of Development

As an obvious extension to Maslow's hierarchy (Wahba, Bridwell, 1976), Erickson proposes eight socio-emotional developmental stages through which a person passes from infancy to late adulthood. As with Maslow (1970), an individual builds upon satisfaction of earlier stages to progress to the successive stages. Erickson (in Pervin, Cervone & John, 2005) defines the stages of development along a continuum in terms of *infancy, toddlership, early childhood, school-age children, adolescence, young adulthood, middle adulthood*, and *maturity or old age*. In infancy, the infant learns *will*. A positive relationship with one's primary caregiver results in trust, security, and a basic sense of optimism. A poorly nurtured child becomes insecure and mistrustful.

In *toddlership*, the individual develops a sense of *Self*. The well-nurtured toddler emerges secure in himself or herself; confident in his or her newfound control, rather than being insecure. In *early childhood*, the young child views family as significant others and role models. The developing child engages in games of imagination and fantasy. A healthy family relationship results in an imaginative child who learns to cooperate with others, and to lead as well as follow. Conversely, a child immobilized by guilt and shame will become fearful, dependent upon others, constrained in development of cooperativeness, and decline to become involved in team play or groups. Significant correlation is found in the establishment of internal or external locus of control.

During *school age*, persons at school and in the neighborhood provide the dominant social influences. To avoid feeling of inferiority, children learn academic and social skills such as reading, writing, arithmetic, and social studies. This argument correlates favorably with *Piaget's States of Intellectual Development*. Piaget (1972, 1990; Renner, Stafford, Lawson, McKinnon, Friot & Kellogg 1976) suggests during the ages from 11-15, thought becomes more abstract; incorporating the principles of formal logic. Additionally, the child develops the functional skills required for life, such as using rules for interacting with peers. The child progresses from free play to rule-based sports and activities. The child who has learned adaptive skills from earlier experiences is trusting, self-directed, and full of initiative. Conversely, the mistrusting child is filled with mistrust and disbelief in the future. The child filled with shame and guilt will experience defeat and inadequacy.

The transition from *adolescence* to adulthood is a transitional period in which one arguably faces the greatest challenges in terms of the range of developmental issues. Havighurst (1952) suggests two of the most important new challenges, and perhaps the most stressful in terms of affect, are *work* and *relationships*. The adolescent develops an identity and a direction for the future, including their future occupation, and the transition from a child in their existing family to head of household in their own families. Peers become the dominant social influence and the adolescents distance themselves from their parents. Adolescents begin experimenting with rebellion and minor delinquency, testing various roles; with any luck finding the one most suitable for them. The adolescent is filled with a continuum of feelings ranging from self-doubt to satisfaction dependent upon the outcome.

The *young adult* distinguishes friendship from love. The successful young adult, for the first time, experiences true intimacy that makes a viable marriage or enduring friendship possible. During *middle-adulthood*, the psychosocial crisis experienced in marriage, parenthood, and the work environment demands *generativity*. The people one lives with and works with become most important during this phase. During *maturity* or *late adulthood*, the other seven psychosocial phases met, the social influence broadens to all humanity. The individual makes peace with his or her strengths and limitations.

Theorists (van der Kolk et al., 1996) suggest trauma results in fixation of perception, cognition, and coping mechanisms at the stage of development in which the trauma occurred. Additionally, the choice of defenses employed by the traumatized individual is influenced by the individual's *developmental stage, temperament,* and *contextual factors* (van der Kolk et al., 1996). Consequently, understanding the age and stage of development at which the trauma was experienced provides an important indicator of the potential predisposition to subsequent retraumatization.

Gender

Van der Kolk et al. (1996) elaborates upon such factors as gender, culture, age, and prior exposure to be strong mediators of PTSS/PTSD development. For example, while fewer women than men experience lifetime traumatic events, women appear to develop PTSD at nearly twice the rate of men (18.3% versus 10.4%) (Gill, Szanton & Page, 2005; Breslau, Reboussin, Anthony & Storr, 2005). Women are also much more likely to experience highly personal traumatic events such as sexual assault, rape, and domestic volence, than their male counterparts are. The personal nature of these events in the midst of fear and helplessness might help explain the higher prevalence of PTSD, as well as maladaptive schema development. Breslau (Breslau, Chilcoat, Kessler, Peterson, & Lucia, 1999) suggest, even after controlling for such variables as prior traumatic experiences, poverty, etc., women are more than twice as likely as men to develop PTSD, and experience PTSS longer than men.

Distinctive differences are found in posttraumatic reactions between males and females. Specifically, males (Scaers, 2001) tend to reenact past trauma assuming the role of the aggressor rather than the victim. Males exposed to adult trauma frequently present with rage and aggressive behavior (i.e., fight or flight). Scaer (2001) offers correlation is found between the level of rage and aggressiveness and whether he had experienced abuse or deprivation as a child. Females, alternatively tend to possess and internal locus of control; manifesting guilt and blaming themselves for the trauma. Thus, women tend to assume a role of helplessness. Scaer (2001) opines females then become increasingly prone to development of revictimization and to be increasingly vulnerable to, and dominated by, abusive men. Whereas males are more apt to engage in a pattern of self-mutilation, female victims tend to engage in less-violent tendencies such as *anorexia nervosa* and *bulimia.* Adult victims of child abuse, in both genders, have a high incidence of dissociation (Scaer, 2001) when faced with adult trauma.

Schema Theory

The fundamental assumption of the schema theory is that the human mind possesses finite processing and storage capabilities. Numerous theorists (Harris, 1998; Pinker, 2002) have engaged in a passionate debate regarding the existence and influence of perceptual, cognitive, and behavioral capabilities resulting from nature and nurture. While some theorists, such as John Locke (in Pinker, 2002) argue for *tabula rasa,* in which humans are provided with a blank slate at birth, other theorists, such as Pervin et al. (2005) argue, as infants, we are innately endowed with a fundamental set of core schemata to enable the survival of mankind. Contemporary theorists (Pinker, 2002) argue, as we evolve from infancy to maturity, we develop a complex schematic system as a roadmap for future interaction with new experiences. These schemas are derived from such natural factors as genetics, biology, and physiology, as well as those learned from sociocultural interaction, spiritual/religious indoctrination, and experiences between self and others.

Vygotsky (1986) suggests child development cannot be fully understood by a study of the individual alone. Rather, we must also examine the external social world in which that individual's life has developed. Through cognitive and communicative functions, children draw upon sociocultural morals, ethics, values, and beliefs, as well as experiences that nurture and scaffold them. Kublin, Wetherby, Crais, and Prizant (1989) support this in their assertion that learning is embedded in the social events occurring as a child interacts with people, objects, and events in the environment. As one ages, he or she assimilates the views of those in which he or she interacts and respects. From micro-to-macro, these influences might be viewed as one's family, peers, and the sociocultural environment in which they interact. Each influences our self-perception, our perception of others, and our reaction to new experiences at diverse junctures.

Early maladaptive schemas result from nature and nurture; the child uses innate personality and temperament to cope with dysfunctional experiences involving parents, siblings, peers, and others during one's early life (Young, 1999). Young argues everyday experiences cumulatively then strengthens the schema. Correlating early childhood behavior with common clinical symptoms, Young (1990, 1994) defined categorical *early maladaptive schemas* (EMSs) and 11 *life traps*, including abandonment, mistrust and abuse, dependence, vulnerability, emotional deprivation, social exclusion, defectiveness, failure, subjugation, unrelenting standards, and entitlement. Without intervention or life-altering experiences, Young suggests these maladaptive schemas developed in childhood continue to unconsciously pervade one's perception, cognition, and behavior throughout their lifetime.

Mental Model

Van der Kolk et al. (1996) questions whether PTSD results from the trauma itself or the subjective interpretation of the experience. Whereas the schema can be considered the tool to enable automaticity when faced with new experiences, the *mental model* is the toolbox. A mental model is a learned process; composed of schemata derived from psychological, physiological, biological, sociological, cultural, and environmental stimuli, which traverse beyond schema theory to include perceptions of task demands and task performances. Initially, our mental model is considered relatively basic. In fact, some consider humans to be born with a blank slate (Pinker, 2002). However, as our knowledge and experience increases, so too does our mental abstraction of our environment. Right or wrong, once recalled, the mental model helps to identify which information is most important for the task, what can be ignored or discarded, and how to interpret that information. Most importantly, a mental model need not be in the conscious mind to influence subsequent cognition and behavior. In some instances, recall may be subconscious and may be applied to a situation without conscious awareness of it.

To understand how humans know, perceive, make decisions, and construct behavior, cognitive researchers have studied mental models in a variety of contexts and environments. Johnson-Laird (1983) proposed mental models as a conceptualization of the deductive reasoning processes resulting from prior experience to view, understand, and solve problems. In terms of the present study, the mental model serves as the model by which one views, understands, and reacts to new experiences in the combat environment. More importantly, it provides the expected outcome based upon existing knowledge. Unfortunately, it also provides the bases for generation of cognitive dissonance by virtue of expected behavior and attribution.

Prior Experience

Van der Kolk et al. (1996) argues many traumatized victims develop a pattern of revictimization. Empirical data offers that rape victims, for example, are more likely than those not previously raped to be raped again. Women and children victimized as children present increased vulnerability to abuse and self-harm later in life. In fact, self-destructive behavior is a common behavior in abused children and adult victims of child abuse. Self-destructive behavior includes such acts as suicide attempts, cutting, and self-starving in addition to reckless endangerment. Van der Kolk (1996) offers that most self-mutilators have childhood history of physical or sexual abuse. Russell (1986) found correlation between childhood victimization and later adolescent and adult alcoholism, substance abuse, and prostitution. Lewis and Balla (1976) and Lewis, Shanok, and Balla (1979) extensively documented the correlation between childhood trauma and subsequent victimization of others.

Cognitive Dissonance

Festinger (1957) asserts that humans have an innate desire for consonance of mind, in which all things make sense. He further argues all people hold specific perceptions and cognitions regarding our environment and ourselves; including our beliefs, attitudes, and behavior. Some theorists (van der Kolk et al., 1996) offer that PTSS/PTSD-evoking experience confronts an individual with behavior in great contrast with his or her existing mental model and associated schemata; this confrontation radically shakes the individual's beliefs and attitudes. Directly applicable to the present case, Abigail is confronted with aspects of human capacity for malevolent behavior greater than the ability of the mind to comprehend. Thus, cognitive dissonance is created between Abigail's mental model of acceptable human behavior and the contrasting experiences.

Client Assessment

Maslow (1970) suggests safety and security rank above all other desires. Among safety and security needs are the need for safety from violence, delinquency, aggressions; moral and physiological security; familial security; and security of health. The need for safety and security being met, the individual ascends to the need for love and belongingness, including such emotionally based needs as friendship, sexual intimacy, and having a family. The absence of these elements, as in Abigail's case, results in susceptibility to loneliness, social anxiety, and depression.

The bases of Abigail's symptoms originate in her childhood experiences. As a child, without sophisticated schemata from which to construct more adaptive schemata, Abigail developed a pattern of fragmentation and repression as a defense mechanism against further psychological and emotional harm to achieve the primary objective—survival. Deprivation of external socialization and the boundary violations by family members, suggest confliction of the needs for safety from aggression; psychological, moral and ethical security; familial security; and the separateness of sex and love.

Many of Abigail's childhood memories, including the most troubling, occurred during this period. Unfortunately, as petite female child, she was incapable of exercising determination or control over her circumstances. Consequently, she adopted a pattern of selective repression to spare herself from harm that was beyond her comprehension and control. This adversely influenced her *Concrete Operations Stage.* Consequently, her mental model consists of maladaptive schemata from which to interact with future experiences. A pattern of boundary violations, cultist activity, and ritualistic sexual abuse acting upon a mental model and associated schemata, constructed on fundamental religious indoctrination, unquestionably provides the necessary elements for extreme cognitive dissonance.

Contextual analysis of Abigail's past and her current illness suggests each of the presented personalities are the result of spontaneous age regression for the purposes of obtaining love and acceptance; establishing and reinforcing core morals, ethics and values; and shaming and punishing Abigail for contradictory behavior. The client suggests her parents routinely engaged in *shaming* as the preferred method of eliciting desired behavior, which would only add to the dissonance. Perceptions, emotions, and behavior that might, otherwise, be considered typical in the normal development of an adolescent girl, such as curiosity of her body and hormonally based emotions, might also be met with cognitive dissonance.

Several assessment instruments are available to assess the validity of the therapists' assertions. A significant link between lifetime traumatic experience and revictimization has expressed by van der Kolk, McFarlane, & Weisaeth (1996) and Scaer (2001, 2005). Lifetime traumatic experiences were assessed using the *Traumatic Life Events Questionnaire* (TLEQ) (Kubany, Haynes, Leisen, Owens, Kaplan, Watson, & Burns, 2000; Kubany, 2004a). The TLEQ is a 25-question self-report instrument requiring 10-15 minutes to administer. This instrument covers a range of commonly assessed childhood and adulthood events. The interview assesses both exposure to the event and individuals' subjective reaction to the event. Assessing the subjective reactions, such as self-reported feelings of terror, horror, or threat to life is necessary for determining whether the event can be considered a criterion A event for PTSD as defined by the *Diagnostic and Statistical Manual of Mental Disorders* (4th ed., text-revised) *(DSM-IV-TR)* (American Psychiatric Association, 2000). Participants use a 7-point response format to indicate frequency of occurrence. Consistent with DSM-IV diagnostic criteria, follow-up probes ask whether respondents felt fear, helplessness, or horror during any event experienced.

PTSD was assessed using the *PTSD Screening and Diagnostic Scale* (PSDS). The PSDS (formerly known as the Distressing Event Questionnaire) is a 38-item self-report inventory that assesses the six DSM-IV criteria for making a diagnosis of PTSD. The PSDS is written at an 8th-grade reading level. Respondents are asked to indicate the degree to which they experience symptoms corresponding to the 17 symptoms of PTSD delineated by the DSM-IV. Respondents are also asked whether they have experienced any symptom for longer than 30 days and, if so, how long. Other items inquire about specific areas of functioning, such as trauma-related anger, guilt, and grief, which provides the basis for PTSD assessment.

Finally, Abigail was asked to complete the 32-item Trauma-Related Guilt Inventory (TRGI), an event-focused self-report measure of trauma-related guilt. The TRGI assesses both cognitive and emotional aspects of guilt associated with a specific traumatic event. Trauma-related guilt was correlated (Kubany, 2004b) with the presence and severity of depression, negative self-esteem, shame, social anxiety, avoidance, and other psychopathological manifestations.

Intervention

Abigail's dissociative symptoms are typical of an adult who experienced early family conflicts, abusive and dysfunctional relationships, and feelings of abandonment (van der Kolk et al., 1996; Scaer, 2001, 2005; Haddock, 2001). In view of the fixation on childhood events and stagnation of coping mechanisms created at the time of the trauma (Bradshaw, 1990), Abigail must be provided the opportunity to recognize and confront, and the skills necessary to excise the demons from her mental model and associated schemata.

Traumatic Incident Reduction (TIR)

Freud (1984) argues, rather that being the result of a single experience, traumatic neuroses often results from the convergence of several traumas, often comparable in nature. Because schemas theoretically build upon previous schemas, this assertion argues that schematic modification must occur in reverse order of development.

Fairbank and Nicholson (1987) then argue regression to the point of the offending trauma is essential to schematic resolution; only those therapeutic techniques that adhere to this assertion have been successful in permanent resolution of posttraumatic stress. Gerbode (1986) affirms the professional consensus of regression to the point of trauma and cognitive restructuring are prerequisites for lasting trauma resolution. Traumatic Incident Reduction (TIR) is a non-hypnotic regressive desensitization therapeutic technique for rapid resolution of posttraumatic stress resulting from such traumatic experiences as combat, violent crime, rape and molestation, childhood sexual abuse, natural disasters, and traumatic bereavement (French & Harris, 1999; Gerbode, 1995).

Practical Application

Following the interview and assessment period (Ross, Heber, Norton, Anderson, Anderson, & Barchet, 1989; Steinberg, 1994) and review of guidelines (Courtois, 1999; American Psychiatric Association, 2000b; American Psychiatric Association, 2004; Fraser, 1997; International Society for the Study of Dissociation, 2004), Abigail was administered *Traumatic Incident Reduction* (TIR) (Gerbode, 1995). TIR is a highly structured client-centered methodology to eliminate the harmful effects associated with past traumatic experiences in a one-on-one, environment with the facilitator (therapist) and the viewer (client). While extensive empirical evidence is available regarding the efficacy of this methodology with persons suffering from posttraumatic stress, the present case is unique in view of the limited clinical application involving persons diagnosed with DID.

The client was advised of extent of confidentiality and signed permission to videotape sessions. In total, five iterations were required to reach the desired endpoint. Discussion of Abigail's concerns and desired outcomes revealed she had experienced perpetually recurring "snapshots" of a particularly troubling event involving her mother.

During the first *viewing,* Abigail was asked to find an incident containing her mother. When asked to approximate when the event occurred, Abigail responded when she was approximately four years old. The client stated that the event occurred in the Western U.S. and occurred during the course of four days. Asked to describe the incident, Abigail became emotionally distressed, rocking and covering her face.

Abigail recalled that she and her mother had traveled to town. She was in the backseat, opposite her mother. She recalled that her mother had picked up a young male child under the premise that his mother had asked her to pick him up. As they left town, the mother drove in an alternate direction from the home of the child. When Abigail stated to her mother that she was not driving in the correct direction, the mother told her to be quiet.

Abigail recalls her mother driving to a wooded area, where she dragged the boy from the car, raised her arm with something long in it, and began beating him. After beating the child, she dragged him back to the station wagon, opened the back, and placed the boy inside. The mother drove to their house. By the time they arrived home, it was dark. Shining the headlights on the woodshed door, she unlocked it and told Abigail to go inside the house and get something to eat while she dragged the boy to the woodshed.

It was dark as Abigail entered the house. She waited in the dark for her mother. She recalled, after some time, the mother came into the house, telling her to go to bed.

The next morning, her mother awakened Abigail. Her mother dressed her, took her downstairs, and fed her. Afterwards, they went outside the woodshed, retrieved the boy's body and her mother buried it in a shallow grave, covering it with lime.

During the second viewing, Abigail was asked to find an incident concerning her mother. Abigail recalls driving to town with her mother. A childhood friend, a boy, was standing in front of the grocery store. The mother motioned for him to come to the car. As the boy approached Abigail's mother stated to him that his mother had asked her to pick him up. The boy got in the front passenger seat. As they drove, Abigail told her mother that she was driving in the wrong direction. They stopped in a wooded clearing. The mother dragged the boy from the car and began beating him. Abigail silently questioned herself, "How can I help him?" She recalled it was becoming dark and she was cold. After the beating, the mother placed the boy in the back and drove home. Abigail recalls the next day; she was taken to a tree in front of the house. People in robes were dancing. She recalled looking down at bulldozer tracks.

During the third viewing, Abigail was asked to find an incident concerning her mother. Abigail recalled sitting in a station wagon on the opposite side of the car from her mother, staring between the seats. Her mother wore bobbed hair with the ends flipping out, a turquoise green summer dress, and black horn-rimmed glasses.

Abigail recalled spotting a childhood friend, a boy, standing in front of a store. The mother motioned for him to come to the car. The mother told him that his mother had asked her to pick him up. As they drove, Abigail told her mother that they were driving in the wrong direction, however was told, "Be quiet." The mother continued to drive down a dirt road. Reaching a clearing, they stopped. The mother began fondling the boy's "private parts," after which she dragged him from the car and began beating him. She threw the boy to the ground and continued beating him. The boy was crying and moaning. It was dark and cold. The mother opened the rear of the station wagon and places the boy inside.

The mother drove home. As she left the car running, she parked to shine the headlights on the woodshed. As she got out to unlock the woodshed, the mother told Abigail to go into the house and get something to eat and said that she will be there in a moment.

As Abigail entered the house, it is dark and she could not reach the food. Consequently, Abigail entered the living room and awaited her mother. As the mother enters the living room, she said, "Why are you sitting in the dark? Get upstairs and go to bed."

Abigail went upstairs and laid on the right side of the bed. The mother came up, and began to read to her. Tired, Abigail turned her back to her mother and tried to sleep. The next morning, Abigail went to the woodshed and huddled in the corner. The boy asked her for help. Abigail was scared because the boy is so pale. Abigail's mother found her in the woodshed. She was dragged into the house and beaten, after which she was given a bath. The water was pink and brown. The mother pulled Abigail from the bathtub, wrapped her with a towel, and taken to bed.

It was dark, as the mother came in and removed Abigail from bed. Unexpectedly, in session, Abigail's normally submissive voice, facial expression, and body language became angry and abusive. Speaking for the first time in first person, an adult female voice said, "Why are you so glum? I don't know what's wrong with you. Why do you have such a sourpuss? Tomorrow is a new day!" [Prolonged period of sobbing and silence]

Returning to her normally submissive past-tense description, Abigail elucidated how her mother dressed her in a blue dress with lace and she wore new shoes. She was taken downstairs and fed at the snack bar in the kitchen. Abigail's mother said, "You're such a good little girl." Abigail, however, did not eat quickly enough. Consequently, the mother grabbed her plate and threw it in the sink. Abigail was dragged from the kitchen into the woodshed. She recalled not wanting to go and being dragged.

Again, Abigail's facial expression and body language reverted to the adult female posture. Speaking in first person, the alter stated, "You see that boy there. That could be you! Do you understand me? Do you understand me?"

The submissive state returning, Abigail stated that she was pulled to the mother. Her mother attempted to comfort her by stroking her hair and stating, "Shush, shush. It's okay. It's okay. Now, now. There, there. Go home and wait. I'll be there in a minute. As Abigail enters the house, it is dark. As the mother enters, she says, "There you are. Why are you sitting in the dark? Come on honey"

Abigail was taken outside, where Abigail heard chanting and singing. She felt sick to her stomach. In session, the uncontrollably sobbing and heavy breathing Abigail, reflects that she dragged her heals. She was taken to a clearing in the woods where there was a bonfire and people in robes chanting.

Beginning the fourth viewing, Abigail was asked to find an incident involving her mother. She reflected that their family was supposed to go to someone's house that evening, so they are driving to town. The mother began calling her "My little priestess."

Inexplicably, speaking in a terrified childlike voice, Abigail relates in first person that there are trees and an area being cleared out. In the middle of a clearing, people in robes are chanting and singing. Among the people are her father, brothers, relatives, and others. She is tossed to the ground, where she sees the boy from the shed lying next to her. She is placed on top of him and the people present begin fondling her privates. She is removed from the boy. Her mother assumes a position on top of the boy and begins sexual gyrations. In session, Abigail crossed her arms and bends forward as if to conceal her breasts.

As the mother got off the boy, Abigail is instructed to nail him to a cross near the bonfire. However, she wasn't strong enough. Abigail was placed on the cross on the opposite side, and the cross is raised. The people were chanting and singing. In session, Abigail begins wailing, sobbing uncontrollably, and elucidation stops. [Prolonged silence]

Asked to find an incident with her mother for the fifth time, Abigail reflected that she had a boy childhood friend; someone nice she could play with. As she and her mother drove to town, Abigail spotted the boy in front of a store. The mother motioned for him to come to the car. The boy entered the car, sitting in the front passenger seat.

As the mother drove, Abigail told her mother that she was driving in the wrong direction. She is told to be quiet. [Much of the previous disclosures are recounted].

As Abigail recounts being taken to the clearing, the adult female voice and posture returned, stating, "What's wrong with you? What's so bad about this? You're a freak! This is fun! Don't you want to have fun Abigail?"

The submissive posture and voice returning, Abigail described a shallow grave. Her mother urinated or defecated in the grave. Following an extended period, the adult female returned, "Think you're like God Abigail? So self-righteous! Little freak! You're not better than us! I hate you! I wish you were dead! Why did I give birth to such a little miscreant?"

The submissive child returning, Abigail described her mother pulling her back to the house and forcing her into the bathtub, during which she hit her head. The water was pink and brown. Abigail is scrubbed hard with a bristle brush, "Oh god, it burns." Her mother washed "her privates equally hard." Abigail was removed from the tub and taken to bed. The mother warned her, "Don't make a sound." Abigail heard laughing coming from the next room, much like a party. Abigail's nephew, who was staying the night, kept peeking in and laughing at her. Abigail laid on the bottom bunk, looking up, and thinking," I wonder how wood is made? Why is it the color it is?" She began thinking, "I wonder what life would be like if I got out of here? Is all of the world like this?" Abigail's breathing becomes labored in session. In a child-like voice she said, "Are they just playing games with me?"

The adult female returning, Abigail angrily says, "Abigail, you are the stupidest child on the face of the earth. I hate you! I wish you were dead!" This explication was followed by extended silence. The host returned stating, "I acted like I agreed with them. I learned to pretend."

In the sixth and final viewing," Abigail recounted seeing the boy in front of the store and his mother motioning to him. The boy was told that his mother wanted her to pick him up. The boy got in, sitting in the front passenger seat. This time, however, Abigail's brother was also in the back seat, behind his mother. As they drive, Abigail told the mother that she was driving in the wrong direction. She is told to be quiet.

The mother drove to the woods and parks. It is dark and cold. The mother leaned over and attempted to perform oral sex on the boy. He, however, protests saying, "No! Stop it!" Abigail's brother is urging the mother on, "Yeah, yeah! Do it!" As the boy tried to resist her, Abigail's mother slapped the boy and scraped him with her fingernails.

Angry, she gets out of the car, dragging him with her. It is cold and beginning to get dark. The mother beat the boy with something long. The mother yelled to her son, "Help me get him into the car." The two placed the boy in the back. The mother drove to their house. Leaving the engine running, the car is positioned to shine the headlights on the shed. The brother got out and opened the door. The boy was carried to the woodshed and the door was shut. Abigail was told to go into the house and get something to eat. She will be in shortly.

The house was dark. Abigail went into the darkened living room across from the television near the fireplace to await her mother. Coming into the living room, Abigail's mother said, "Go to bed." Shortly, the mother comes upstairs to read to her. Tired, Abigail turned her back to her mother and tried to sleep.

The next morning, Abigail went downstairs, sitting at the snack bar to eat cereal. Afterwards, Abigail went outside to play. Her mother reminded Abigail to stay away from the woodshed. Wanting to see her friend, Abigail sneaked into the shed. However, Abigail's mother found her there, dragged her to the house, and beat her. Abigail was taken to the bathroom, forced into the bathtub. She hit her head. The water was pink and brown. Abigail's mother dressed her in a light fall dress with lace. Her father and brothers are gone.

Abigail is taken to the kitchen and fed, however was taking too long. The mother grabbed the plate and threw it into the sink. Abigail was dressed in a robe. Grabbed by the arm, she was dragged outside toward the clearing in the woods. In the clearing, people in robes chanted and sang. Abigail's friend lay on the ground. She was tossed down next to him. A bonfire burned in the center, not far from a cross.

In session, Abigail crossed her legs in a more relaxed posture, rocking her left foot in a rhythmic motion. She reflected that the people removed the boy's clothes, while others danced and sang. Abigail was grabbed next. Her tights and underwear were removed and she was forced on top of the boy. She felt nauseous. Members of the group began stimulating her genitals. Someone yelled, "Don't you like the boy. Don't you want to be his?"

She was lifted from the ground and instructed to tie him to the cross. Someone says, "She's too weak." She is pushed aside as the boy is tied to the cross. Abigail was also tied to the cross and it was hoisted. The crowds become very solemn, singing some sort of chant. The cross was lowered and the boy placed in a shallow grave. The mother urinated or defecated into the grave. Abigail recalled saying, "He's cold. Can't I get him a blanket?" However, the mother replies "Don't worry about him! He's a pig." Abigail was taken to the house and tossed into the bathtub. Her mother scrubbed her hard with a brush. She is told to go to bed. Abigail recalls a lonely feeling… [Silence]

Asked to recall an incident involving her mother for the sixth time, Abigail, in session, opened her eyes, laughed briefly and said, "I can't." The session, from the first iteration to reaching a satisfactory endpoint had lasted three hours and ten minutes.

Post-viewing, Abigail presented a relaxed posture and laughed; despite the fact, neither the facilitator nor therapist had ever previously seen her do so. Abigail demonstrated a remarkably increased range of affect. Abigail relates her experience in session was as if she was watching herself from the outside and that someone else was talking. Abigail expressed a great sense of relief not having to hide the events any longer.

The following day, Abigail related that she had slept hard the afternoon and night following the session, awaking late the following morning. Additional details had come into view. She expressed that she recalls processing a "flood of memories." This time, however, she did not fear them. A day later, Abigail reflects that she had "made peace" with the dead childhood friend and felt joy for the first time upon waking.

Abigail expressed that she had begun to experience new revelations, such as she liked rock music when she never had previously. As Abigail continued, she related that, for the first time in memory, she was able to go into a grocery store without apprehension and complete the transaction without embarrassing herself. She also stated she felt increased energy for such tasks as cleaning the house. In short, Abigail stated her current state was "remarkable." She did state, however, she now has more questions that she had never previously contemplated for which she needs answers.

Schema Therapy

As a final goal, the victim should engage in behavioral change by gradually learning to trust people, increasing interpersonal intimacy, and sharing memories, thoughts and feelings of abuse with others. Groups such as Parents United against Child Sexual Abuse (http://www.lfsneb.org/counselingandaddiction/sexualabuse/support/index.asp), Adults Molested as Children United (AMAC), Daughters and Sons United, and other such support groups provide an exceptional venue for victims and their families as well as providing a safe and supportive environment for offenders, victims, families, and supporters to discuss childhood sexual abuse. Ideally, through the lessons learned in such environments, sexual abuse recidivism and the sexual abuse cycle between victim and offender will be broken. Through such interaction, information regarding the patterns, cycles, beliefs, and behavior associated with childhood sexual abuse is provided and victims learn skills to set and enforce limits with abusive people. A positive outcome such programs is the ability of all participants to become more aware and less judgmental when people make mistakes in general.

Dr. Young (1990, 1999) suggests three experiential steps for the treatment of sexual abuse: 1) Recall memories of abuse/humiliation; 2) express anger, and; 3) find a safe place away from the abuser. Dr. Young (1990, 1999; Young & Klosko, 1993, 1994; Young, Klosko & Weishaar, 2003) also recommends a six-step cognitive phase, which includes: 1) reduce hypervigilence to the abuse; 2) alter the misperception or fear of others as being ill-intentioned, abusive, manipulative, or dishonest; 3) alter self-blame for the abuse; 4) label the abuse accordingly (i.e., don't make excuses for the abuser); 5) alter the view of helplessness, and finally; 6) teach a spectrum of mistreatment as a continuum from right to wrong.

In essence, schema-focused cognitive behavioral therapy consists of helping individuals identify, challenge, and contradict maladaptive schemata and helping them develop adaptive schemata.

Applicability of Theories to other Groups

In conceptualization, this learner suggests that much of the human perception, cognition, and ultimately behavior are derived from the *schema theory*. *Schemata* refer to prototypical abstractions for interacting with new experiences evolving from the cohesion of abstract facts and prior experience. Schemata then evolve from a simplistic methodology for a discrete encounter into more elaborately organized schemata for addressing a myriad of related and seemingly unrelated experiences. Accurate or not, schemata then provide a methodology to perceive, assess, understand, and react to new experiences without the need to learn all of the associated objects, relationships, and assess risk each time a similar experience is encountered (Rivera, 1991).

As executive agents, *mental models* extend beyond schema theory to include perceptions of task demands and provide an abstraction of how to achieve the task objectives. Once recalled, the mental model helps identify the most important information necessary to achieve the objective, including task conceptualization. More importantly, because of the finite human capacity to receive, process, and store information, the mental model provides a methodology for data interpretation, and assesses which can be ignored or discarded. Resultantly, the mental model is the core mechanism from which our reaction or behavior is evoked.

Perhaps the most salient aspect of the mental model and schema theories is the belief that the human mind strives for *consonance.* Festinger (1957) suggests people are innately endowed with the need for cognitive consistency (consonance) in their morals, ethics, values, and beliefs.

The *Theory of Reasoned Action* (TRA) suggests people intend to behave in a manner that allows them to achieve favorable outcomes and meet the expectation of others (Ajzen & Fishbein, 1980). Behavioral intention is the product of 1) the person's attitude toward the behavior, which includes behavioral beliefs concerning the potential outcomes of the behavior and positive or negative evaluation of the possible outcomes, and; 2) subjective norms, which include the perception of the sociocultural pressure to perform the behavior.

Consequently, one might then conceptualize that dissociative reaction to a single traumatic experience might then be the foundational basis for a generalized schema for coping with a myriad of experiences in which cognitive dissonance is reached (Gold, 2000), irrespective of sociocultural, religious, or other categorical groupings.

This learner suggests, however, that mental disorder diagnosis is, in fact, highly correlated to the population in which the individual interacts (American Psychiatric Association. 2000a). Castillo (1997) suggests dissociative disorders are culturally bound. The DSM-IV-TR (American Psychiatric Association, 2000a) suggests objective assessment is imperative because dissociative states are strongly correlated to the acceptable expression of sociocultural activity and religious practice.

When looking to mental health diagnoses, then, it is important for the diagnostician to understand that it is not sufficient to merely understand the sociocultural factors within the environment in which the individual in question currently resides. Rather, one must be well versed in sociocultural, religious, and folk beliefs, which the individual has integrated to formulate their individual mental model and associated schema. For example, the automatic diagnosis of dissociative disorder in a recently arrived Hispanic or Far Eastern person, as well as many Native American individuals, would be wholly inappropriate because of sociocultural and religious beliefs in the dissociative self as a matter of accepted practice.

The practice of Sufism, a mystic school of thought related to Islam views dissociative behavior as an acceptable practice. In fact, a large part of Muslim literature comes from the Sufis, who created great books of poetry (e.g., *1001 Arabian Nights* and the *Rubaiyat of Omar Khayyam*). Both of these writings contain the profound teachings of the Sufis that are largely incomprehensible to many American and European scholars because of their Westernized mental model. Drawing from Qur'anic verses, for example, virtually all Sufis distinguish between *Nafs, Qalb, Sirr,* and *Ruh.* These concepts designate various psycho-spiritual *organs* or, sometimes, faculties of sensory and supersensory perception. One endeavoring to understand the Sufi schema must then look to the practices of *philosophical hermeneutics, scriptural hermeneutics,* and *phenomenology.*

Hermeneutics is largely the result of the 18th Century Prussian theologian and philosopher Friedrich Schleiermacher, who was for a time himself a student of Immanuel Kant. (i.e., the founder of the Kantian Theory). Schleiermacher's theory is grounded in the belief that there is no absolute mind or absolute body.

Schleirmacher conceptualizes a dualism of *ego* and *non-ego*; the ego being itself body and soul. The functions of the ego are seen to be are either functions of the senses or functions of the intellect (Watkins & Watkins, 1988; 1997). The function of senses consists of two classes: *perception* (objective) and *feeling* (subjective).

Likewise, functions of intellect are seen as consisting of two classes: *cognition* and *volition*, with both being the function of thought. Schleiermacher suggests that behind both ego and non-ego is the self-consciousness—the third form of thought. Self-consciousness is always present and is both objective (e.g., non-ego) and subjective (e.g., consciousness of ourselves). The non-ego is conceptualized to be the controlling agent, which helps, hinders, enables, or disenables. Through non-ego, we feel pleasure or pain. As such, integration of larger ideas into consciousness produces aesthetic, moral, and religious feelings. This learner opines, the dissonance of these fundamental elements of our mental model the causal agent of dissociative disorders resulting from cognitive dissonance.

As suggested by Schleiermacher, religious feeling is the highest form of thought and of life. Accordingly, it is suggested that the individual mental model is replete with sociocultural, religious, and experiential underpinnings that would greatly influence the development, diagnosis, and treatment of dissociative disorders.

The Holy Bible, the Tanakh, the Torah, the Theravada, Sutra, and the non-Wahhabist interpretation of the Qur'an—the predominant religious texts in Western and Far East civilizations -- are largely pacifistic. Consequently, this learner suggests ritualistic ideation of trauma within the Western civilization, which are not typically acclimated to violence and trauma, is perhaps the result of the human mind at dissonance with the theological underpinnings with God's benevolence. In essence then, one might conceptualize that the individual, believing in the ethicality and morality expressed in many Western and Far East religions, would experience such dissonance with the egregious infliction of trauma. Resultantly, they would seek refuge beyond their existing mental model as an unintentional schema to reach consonance with their spiritual being, resulting in dissociative disorder (Rosik, 2004).

Conclusions and Recommendations

In Abigail's case, it is envisioned that she experienced extreme dissonance, anxiety, and psychological and emotional distress as she evaluated the positive and negative outcomes of acceptance or rejection the egoistic and often unnatural desires of others in relationship to her own self-needs and desires.

Clearly, Abigail adopted the schema of sexual submissiveness. Arguably, this schema was adopted as a learned behavior; perhaps to achieve favorable outcome, or to overcome fear of abandonment. As her environment became increasingly isolated, her sociocultural interaction became increasingly myopic.

It is suggested, with the purported sexual abuse, Abigail's perception of interfamilial relationships and sociocultural norms and expectations became increasingly convoluted as well.

Consequently, Abigail might have learned that sexual gratification of others as being equated to desirable outcome (e.g., perceived affection and improved relationships). However, the cognitive dissonance created by behavior contradictory to her strong spiritual beliefs would have simultaneously resulted in negative self-perception.

Thus, the psychodynamics experienced would have resulted in psychological and emotional distress in which she would have viewed her behavior on two counter-opposing levels; one favorable and one unfavorable, potentially resulting in dissociative disorder (Kluft, 1995; Coons, 1984; Coons, Bowman, & Milstein, 1988; Bowman, & Markand, 1996; Carlson, 1997; Carlson & Putnam, 1993; Carlson, Putnam, Ross, Torem, Coons, Dill, Loewenstein, & Braun, 1993; Dunn, Ryan, & Paolo, & Miller, 1993; Dietrich, 2003; McCauley, Kern, Kolodner, Schroeder, DeChant, Ryden, Derogatis, & Bass, 1997; Van der Kolk, Perry, & Herman, 1991).

Employing the psychodynamic model, therapists conducted Traumatic Incident Reduction (TIR) intervention, resulting in favorable outcome. Subsequent study, however, is needed to establish reliability.

References

Ajzen, I. & Fishbein, M. (1980). *Understanding the attitudes and predicting social behavior.* Englewood Cliffs, New Jersey: Prentice-Hall Inc.

American Psychiatric Association. (2000a). *Diagnostic and statistical manual of mental disorders* (4th ed.) Text Revision. Washington, DC: Author.

American Psychiatric Association. (2000b). *Statement on therapies focused on memories of childhood physical and sexual abuse.* Washington, DC: Author.

American Psychiatric Association (2004). Practice guidelines for the treatment of patients with Acute Stress Disorder (ASD) and Posttraumatic Stress Disorder (PTSD). *American Journal of Psychiatry 161*(supplement), 1-57.

Armstrong, J.G. (1991). The psychological organization of Multiple Personality Disordered patients as revealed in psychological testing. *Psychiatric Clinics of North America, 7,* 135-148.

Bradshaw, J. (1990). Homecoming: Reclaiming and championing your inner child. New York: Bantam Books.

Bowman, E.S., & Markand, O.N. (1996). Psychodynamics and psychiatric diagnoses of pseudoseizure subjects. *American Journal of Psychiatry, 153,* 57-63.

Bremner, J.D., Southwick, S.M., Johnson, D.J., Yehuda, R., Charney, D.S. (1993). Childhood physical abuse and combat-related posttraumatic stress disorder in Vietnam veterans. *American Journal of Psychiatry, 150,* 235-239.

Brenner, I. (1999). Deconstructing DID. *American Journal of Psychotherapy, 53*(3), 344-360.

Breslau, N., Chilcoat, H.D., Kessler, R.C., Peterson, E.L., & Lucia, V.C. (1999) Vulnerability to assaultive violence: Further specification of the sex difference in posttraumatic stress disorder. *Psychological Medicine 29,* 813-821.

Breslau, N., Davis, G.C., & Andreski, P. (1995). Risk factors for PTSD-related traumatic events: a prospective analysis. *American Journal of Psychiatry, 152,* 529-535.

Breslau, N., Reboussin, B.A., Anthony, J.C., & Storr, C.L. (2005). *Archives of General Psychiatry, 62,* 1343-1351.

Carlson, E.B. (1997). *Trauma assessments: A clinician's guide.* New York: Guilford Press.

Carlson, E.B., & Putnam, F.W. (1993). An update on the Dissociative Experiences Scale. *Dissociation, 6,* 16-27.

Carlson, E.B., Putnam, F.W., Ross, C.A., Torem, M., Coons, P.M., Dill, D., Loewenstein, R.J., & Braun, B.G. (1993). Validity of the Dissociative experiences scale in screening for Multiple Personality Disorder: A multicenter study. *American Journal of Psychiatry, 150,* 1030-1036.

Castillo, R.J. (1997). *Culture and mental illness.* Pacific Grove, CA: Brooks/Cole.

Chu, J.A. (1988). Ten traps for therapists in the treatment of trauma survivors. *Dissociation, 1*(4), 24-32.

Chu, J.A. (1998). *Rebuilding shattered lives: The responsible treatment of complex posttraumatic and dissociative disorders.* New York: John Wiley & Sons.

Chu, J.A. (2005). *The guidelines for treating dissociative identity disorder in adults.* Retrieved June 13, 2006 from http://www.issd.org/indexpage/treatguideref.htm

Chu, J.A., Frey, L.M., Ganzel, B.L., & Matthews, J.A. (1999). Memories of childhood abuse: Dissociation, amnesia and corroboration. *American Journal of Psychiatry, 156,* 749-755.

Comer, R.J. (2004). *Abnormal psychology* (5th ed.). New York: Worth.

Coons, P.M. (1984). The differential diagnosis of Multiple Personality Disorder: A comprehensive review. *Psychiatric Clinics of North America, 7,* 51-67.

Coons, P. M. (1986). Treatment progress in 20 patients with Multiple Personality Disorder. *Journal of Nervous and Mental Disease, 174,* 715-721.

Courtois, C.A. (1999). *Recollections of sexual abuse: Treatment principles and guidelines.* New York: W.W. Norton & Co.

Dell, P.F. (2002). Dissociative phenomenology of Dissociative Identity Disorder. *Journal of Nervous and Mental Disease, 190,* 1-15.

Dietrich, A. (2003). Characteristics of child maltreatment, psychological dissociation, and somatoform dissociation of Canadian inmates. *Journal of Trauma & Dissociation, 4*(1), 81-100.

Draijer, N., & Boon, S. (1999). The imitation of Dissociative Identity Disorder: Patients at risk, therapists at risk. *Journal of Psychiatry & Law, 27,* 423-458.

Dunn, G.E., Ryan, J.J., & Paolo, A.M., & Miller, D. (1993). Screening for MPD: Clinical utility of the Questionnaire of Experiences of Dissociation. *Dissociation, 6,* 38-41.

Engel, G.L. (1977). The need for a new medical model: a challenge for biomedicine. *Science, 196*(4286), 129-136.

Engel, G.L. (1980). The clinical application of the biopsychosocial model. *The American Journal of Psychiatry, 137*(5), 535-544.

Festinger, L. (1957). *A theory of cognitive dissonance.* Stanford, CA: Stanford University Press.

Fraser, G.A. (Ed.). (1997). *The dilemma of ritual abuse: Cautions and guides for therapists.* Washington, DC: American Psychiatric Press.

French, G.D., & Harris, C.J. (1999). *Traumatic incident reduction (TIR).* Boca Raton, FL: CRC Press.

Freud, S. (1970). *A general introduction to psychoanalysis.* New York: Simon & Schuster.

Freud, S. (1984). *Two short accounts of psychoanalysis.* In J. Strachey (Tr.), Five lectures on psychoanalysis (p. 37). Singapore: Penguin Books.

Gerbode, F.A. (1995). *Beyond psychology: An introduction to metapsychology* (3rd ed.). Menlo Park, CA: Institute for Research in Metapsychology.

Gill, J.M., Szanton, S.L., & Page, G.G. (2005). Biological underpinnings of health alterations in women with PTSD: a sex disparity. *Biological Research for Nursing, 7,* 44-54.

Gold, S.N. (2000). *Not trauma alone: Therapy for child abuse survivors in family and social context.* Philadelphia: Brunner/Routledge.

Haddock, D.B. (2001). *Dissociative identity disorder sourcebook.* New York: Contemporary Books.

Harris, J.R. (1998). *The nurture assumption.* New York: Free Press

Havighurst, R. J. (1952). *Developmental tasks and education.* New York: David McKay.

International Society for the Study of Dissociation. (2004). Guidelines for the evaluation and treatment of dissociative symptoms in children and adolescents. *Journal of Trauma & Dissociation, 5*(3), 119-150.

Johnson-Laird, P. N. (1983*). Mental models: Towards a cognitive science of language, inference, and consciousness.* Cambridge, MA: Harvard University Press.

Kluft, R.P. (1988). The phenomenology and treatment of extremely complex Multiple Personality Disorder. *Dissociation, 1*(4), 47-58.

Kluft, R.P. (1989). Playing for time: temporizing techniques in the treatment of Multiple Personality Disorder. *American Journal of Clinical Hypnosis, 32,* 90-98.

Kluft, R.P. (1990). Incest and subsequent revictimization: The case of therapist-patient sexual exploitation, with a description of the sitting duck syndrome. In R.P. Kluft (Ed.), *Incest-related syndromes of adult psychopathology* (pp. 263-287). Washington, DC: American Psychiatric Press.

Kluft, R.P. (1995). The confirmation and disconfirmation of memories of abuse in Dissociative Identity Disorder patients: A naturalistic study. *Dissociation, 8,* 253-258.

Kluft, R.P., & Fine, C.G. (Eds.). (1993). *Clinical perspectives on Multiple Personality Disorder.* Washington, DC: American Psychiatric Press.

Kublin, K. S., Wetherby, A. M., Crais, E. R., & Prizant, B. M. (1989). Prelinguistic dynamic assessment: A transactional perspective. In A. M. Wetherby, S. F. Warren, & J. Reichle (Eds.), *Transitions in prelinguistic communication* (pp. 285-312). Baltimore, MD: Paul H. Brookes.

Lewis, D.O. & Balla, D. A. (1976). *Delinquency & Psychopathology.* New York: Grune & Stratton.

Lewis, D. O., Shanok, S.S., & Balla, D. A. (1979). Parental criminality and medical histories of delinquent children. *American Journal of Psychiatry, 136,* 288-292.

Lewis, D.O., Yeager, C.A., Swica, Y., Pincus, J.H., & Lewis, M. (1997). Objective documentation of child abuse and dissociation in 12 murderers with Dissociative Identity Disorder. *American Journal of Psychiatry, 154,* 1703-1710.

Loftus, E. & Hoffman, H. (1989). Misinformation and memory: The creation of new memories. *Journal of Experimental Psychology: General, 118,* 199-104.

Loftus, E., Joslyn, S., & Polage, D. (1998). Repression: A mistaken impression? *Development and Psychopathology, 10(4),* 781-792.

Loftus, E., & Ketcham, K. (1994). The myth of repressed memories: False accusations and allegations of sexual abuse. New York: St. Martin's Press.

Maslow, A. H. (1943). *A Theory of Human Motivation.* Psychological Review, 50, 370-396.

Maslow, A. H. (1970). *Motivation and Personality* (2nd ed.), New York, Harper & Row

McCauley, J., Kern, D.E., Kolodner, K., Schroeder, A.F., DeChant, H.K., Ryden, J., Derogatis, L., & Bass, E.B. (1997). Clinical characteristics of women with a history of childhood abuse: Unhealed wounds. *Journal of the American Medical Association, 277,* 1362-1368.

Murphy, P.E. (1994). Dissociative experiences and dissociative disorders in a non-clinical university student group. *Dissociation, 7(1),* 28-34.

Paniagua, F.A. (2001). *Diagnosis in a multicultural context.* Thousand Oaks, CA: Sage.

Perry, B. D. (2002). Childhood experience and the expression of genetic potential: What childhood neglect tells us about nature and nurture. *Brain and Mind, 3,* 79-100.

Pervin, L. A., Cervone, D., & John, O. P. (2005). *Personality: Theory and research* (9th ed.). New York: John Wiley & Sons.

Piaget, J. (1972). *The psychology of the child.* New York: Basic Books.

Piaget, J. (1990). *The child's conception of the world.* New York: Littlefield Adams.

Pinker, Steven (2002). *The blank slate: The modern denial of human nature* (337-371). New York: Viking Penguin.

Renner, J., Stafford, D., Lawson, A., McKinnon, J., Friot, E., & Kellogg, D. (1976). *Research, teaching, and learning with the Piaget model.* Norman, OK: University of Oklahoma Press.

Rivera, M. (1991). Multiple personality disorder and the social system: 185 cases. *Dissociation, 4,* 79-82.

Rosik, C.H. (2004). Possession Phenomena in North America: A case study with ethnographic, psychodynamic, religious, and clinical implications. *Journal of Trauma & Dissociation, 5(1),* 49-76.

Ross, C.A. (1991). Epidemiology of Multiple Personality Disorder and dissociation. *Psychiatric Clinics of North America, 14,* 503-517.

Ross, C.A., Heber. S., Norton, G.R., Anderson, D., Anderson, G., & Barchet. P. (1989). The Dissociative Disorders Interview Schedule: A structured interview. *Dissociation, 2*(3), 169-218.

Scaer, R.C. (2001). *The body bears the burden: Trauma, dissociation, and disease.* Binghamton, NY: The Hayworth Medical Press.

Scaer, R.C. (2005). *The trauma spectrum: Hidden wounds and human resiliency.* New York: W.W. Norton.

Steinberg, M. (1994). *Structured Clinical Interview for DSM-IV Dissociative Disorders - Revised (SCID-D-R)* (2nd ed.). Washington, DC: American Psychiatric Press.

van der Kolk, B.A., MacFarlane, A.C., Weisaeth, L. (1996). *Traumatic stress: The effects of overwhelming experience on the mind.* New York: The Guilford Press.

Vygotsky, L. (1986). *Thought and language.* Boston: MIT Press.

Vygotsky, L., & Vygotsky, S. (1980). *Mind in society: The development of higher psychological processes.* Cambridge: Harvard University Press.

Wahba, M. A., Bridwell, L. G. (1976). Maslow reconsidered: A review of research on the need hierarchy theory. *Organizational Behavior and Human Performance, 15,* 212-240.

Waller, N.G., Putnam, F.W., & Carlson, E.B. (1996). Types of dissociation and dissociative types: A taxometric analysis of dissociative experiences. *Psychological Methods, 1,* 300-321.

Watkins, J.G., & Watkins, H.H. (1988). The management of malevolent ego states in Multiple Personality Disorder. *Dissociation, 1*(1), 67-78.

Watkins, J.G., & Watkins, H.H. (1997). *Ego states: Theory and therapy.* New York: W.W. Norton & Co.

Watson, J.B., & Raynor, R. (1920). Little emotional Albert. In R.R. Hock, *Forty studies that changed psychology* (pp. 71-76). Upper Saddle River, NJ: Pearson Prentice Hall.

Young, J.E. (1990, 1999). *Cognitive therapy for personality disorders: A schema-focused approach* (Revised Edition). Sarasota, Florida: Professional Resource Press.

Young, J.E. & Klosko, J.S. (1993, 1994). *Reinventing your life.* New York: Plume Books.

Young, J.E., Klosko, J.S., & Weishaar, M. (2003). *Schema therapy: A practitioner's guide.* Guilford Publications: New York.

Pandemics and Biological/Chemical Terrorism Attacks:

A New Role for Disaster Mental Health

Thom Curtis, Ph.D.

The threat of an avian influenza pandemic has forced the health care system of the United States to reexamine its capability to respond to a sudden, overwhelming demand for services. Researchers2 have been consistent in their conclusions that most American medical systems do not have sufficient resources to adequately meet the surge in demand expected in the event of a pandemic or bioterrorism attack.

Billions of dollars have been spent preparing for such events in the five years since the attacks of September 11, 2001 and the mailing of letters containing anthrax to politicians and media outlets in Florida, New York and Washington, DC (Lurie, Valdez, Wasserman, Stoto, Myers, Molander, Asch, Mussington, & Solomon, 2004). The Center for Biosecurity at the University of Pittsburgh reported that even with these increased benefits, "hospitals' capacity to absorb an unexpected surge of patients from an attack- or and epidemic-has not improved because relatively little money has been spent on that aspect ((Mackenzie, 2006, p. 21)."

It is expected that announcement of a pandemic disease or a bioterrorism attack will overwhelm the health systems' ability to respond to the crush of people seeking medical aid. There are approximately 5,756 hospitals in the United States. Together they have about 946,997 beds available. On an average day, over two-thirds of those beds are occupied (AHA, 2005). Epidemiologists predict that during a pandemic outbreak of avian influenza, as many as 5.8 million Americans will require hospitalization. While the disease is expected to hit in waves and not all those infected will require hospitalization at the same time, one does not need complex mathematics to recognize that there will not be sufficient additional beds in the system to meet even a fraction of the increased demand.

To further compound this problem, previous experience with similar events indicates that those who are truly ill or have been exposed will be greatly outnumbered by multitudes of fearful, unexposed citizens who will unnecessarily seek treatment. A major roadblock to a successful response to either emergency is a lack of trained professionals to deal with the numbers attempting to access medical services unnecessarily.

This paper describes the prospects of overwhelming demand for services and a proposal that mental health professionals can be cross-trained to assist medical professionals in some phases of the emergency response.

---

2 I have found it virtually impossible to keep up with the volume of research that has been and is being published regarding preparations for a pandemic or bioterrorism attack. Most of these publications detail the inability of the U.S. health care system to cope with either eventuality. Many provide general categories of attention that is required and outline protocols that need to be developed, but few provide detailed descriptions of how public health systems and hospitals can operationalize the theoretical proposals.

Surge Capacity

The Agency for Healthcare Research and Quality (AHRQ) of the U. S. Department of Health and Human Services (2006) defined surge capacity as "a health care system's ability to expand quickly beyond normal services to meet an increased demand for medical care in the event of bioterrorism or other large-scale public health emergencies (p. 1)." The Nevada Health Association (2006) added detail to the definition:

> Hospital surge capacity refers to the ability of a health care system to provide appropriate medical care and treatment for a markedly increased volume of patients based on the situation. This term "capacity" is a metric that specifically measures the volume of patients that can be accommodated, and is not a metric that measures the quality of service, patient care services or medical capabilities (p.5).

Hospital facilities in the United States have most of their facilities in use most of the time. There are not lots of empty hospital beds or unused emergency capacity anywhere in the country. It will be difficult to suddenly produce additional beds, equipment or staff if there is a widespread emergency that pushes the system's capacity with sick and dying patients. Tommy Thompson, former secretary of the United States Department of Health and Human Services, described one aspect of surge capacity. "The just-in-time economy is really the enemy for getting prepared for a pandemic. We have 100,000 ventilators, and 85,000 are in use daily. What happens if we have a pandemic? You don't just call someone and say deliver another 50,000 (Seeman, 2005)."

A 2004 study (Lurie, et al) of seven health care regions in California representing about 39% of the state's population, found that only "one jurisdiction had comprehensively assessed surge capacity" and "one jurisdiction had well-developed plans to handle the worried-well" (p.40). This and other studies indicate that while surge capacity and problems dealing with the worried-well are recognized at a theoretical level, there is still a considerable shortfall in meeting those needs.

The federal government has recognized that the lack of surge capacity is not isolated to California. The Health Resources and Services Administration (HRSA) of the United States Department of Health and Human Services (DHHS) is responsible for assisting health care systems across the country to prepare for emergencies such as bioterrorism attacks or pandemics. HRSA has taken the lead along with the Center for Disease Control (CDC) in recognizing and defining the need for surge capacity throughout the U.S.

Following most natural disasters and terror attacks, impacted communities can expect help from outside the impact area. Depending on the size and type of the catastrophe, help and additional medical resources may take a while to arrive. However, impacted communities can rely on the fact that outside help will eventually come. Woodson (2006b) points out that when an influenza pandemic strikes, the problems of surge capacity will be aggravated by the likelihood that infectious outbreaks will affect many different locations simultaneously. There may not be any outside help available.

A further surge capacity variable contemplated by many emergency planners concerns willingness of health care workers to report to work during a pandemic or bioterrorism incident. Surveys have shown that a portion of workers will not report because of fears of becoming infected themselves or they will be unwilling to take the risk of spreading the infection to their families.

"Worried Well"

Research indicates that the "surge capacity" of health systems will be tested not only by those who are in genuine need of medical treatment during such an event, but by multitudes of "worried well" who will present with or without symptoms at medical facilities. Numerous research papers have been published in medical journals over the past decade addressing the need for health care facilities to prepare for surges of demand during catastrophic situations.

During the morning rush hour on March 20, 1995, the Japanese religious sect Aum Shinrikyo released the deadly nerve agent, sarin gas, on five Tokyo commuter trains. Twelve commuters died from exposure to the gas, 54 were seriously injured and about 980 others were sufficiently exposed to require medical attention. Civil defense and emergency medical professionals around the world have learned many lessons from these attacks and their aftermath[3]. Among the most significant was that 5,500 people rushed to hospitals for treatment. For every one person who was exposed to the gas and required medical attention, four non-exposed citizens arrived at medical facilities and expected treatment. The difficulty sorting out the ill from the simply panicked delayed medical treatment for those who really needed it (Beaton, Stergachis, Oberle, ridges, Nemuth, & Thomas, 2005; Olson, 1999; Taneda, 2005).

Similar patterns have been noted following virtually every incident in which some portion of the public has been exposed to toxic or infectious agents (either natural or human induced). The number of people believing they have been exposed and seeking treatment far surpasses those actually at risk. The flood of "worried well" overwhelms the ability of the health care system to determine who is sick or may have been exposed and would benefit from immediate treatment.

In 2003, hospitals in Toronto, Ontario, Canada were swarmed by people fearing exposure to the Severe Acute Respiratory Syndrome (SARS) virus. Final analysis indicated there were only 438 confirmed cases of SARS in Toronto resulting in 44 deaths. Hospital facilities were barraged by people seeking medical assistance who had not been exposed to someone with an infection. Coming to a hospital that was treating actual SARS patients actually exposed them to the risk of contacting the disease. It was decided to resort to a telephone hotline system which handled approximately 300,000 calls during a four month period from March to June 2003 (Bogdan, 2004).

The SARS virus was spread to Canada by people traveling from infected regions of Asia. Hospitals throughout Asia experienced the same panic as those in Toronto. A hotline was established in Taipei, Taiwan, to screen people who feared they were infected. Using body temperatures and other selected symptoms, it was determined that less than one percent of those who thought they had SARS exhibited actual symptoms and needed to be further

---

[3] In addition to recognition of the "worried well" phenomenon, civil defense and medical professionals took note of public communication difficulties, operational logistics problems such as transportation and surge capacity, and secondary exposure risks of emergency responders and hospital personnel. See Beaton, Stergachis, Oberle, Bridges, Nemuth, & Thomas, 2005, for details of lessons learned from the Tokyo sarin gas attacks.

screened by medical professionals (Kaydos-Daniels, Olowokure, Chang, Barwick, Deng, Lee, Kuo, Su, Chen, & Maloney, 2004).

Evans, Crutcher, Shadle, Clements and Bronze (2002) pointed out that these "worried well" consume limited resources and interfere with access to needed assistance by critically ill patients who were exposed. A number of different plans have been proposed to enable medical facilities to deal with the rush of patients expected. Some of these plans include protocols for determining appropriate treatment for each patient depending on their exposure to the infectious agent or symptoms that are observed. These "triage" protocols provide excellent outlines for handling each case. The shortcoming recognized in many plans is the lack of trained personnel to both triage the masses of sick or "worried well" and at the same time provide the necessary intensive treatment required by those who can be saved.

As health care facilities mobilize to meet the medical needs of individuals who have been injured or infected by the event, they will be overwhelmed by a rush of individuals who have heard about the catastrophe and believe that they are also in need of medical attention. Some will present with physical symptoms similar to those of actual victims as described in the media even though they were not someplace impacted by the event. Others who were not in the impact area present with various stress-related symptoms or no symptoms at all, but express fear of exposure and the desire for prophylactic treatment just in case they might have been infected.

Under most existing systems, the professionals who are responsible for sorting the genuinely afflicted from those who are experiencing anxiety or non-event related symptoms are the same people who are needed to provide desperately needed treatment to the ill or injured. The entire system faces gridlock as the number of people requiring emergency treatment approaches the medical facility's capacity and new casualties continue to arrive mixed among throngs of the "worried well".

In order to effectively assist in the triage effort, mental health professionals need to understand the "worried-well" phenomenon. In a publication for military commanders, Fran Pilch (2003) divides the "worried-well" into three categories:

> The first are those who experience symptoms of the disease in question, or generalized symptoms, but who do not have the disease. These individuals may not have been exposed in any real way, and yet they are genuinely convinced that they are ill. This group would include those who experience physiological symptoms as a consequence of heightened fear, alertness, or feelings of helplessness. The second group consists of those who are anxious about potentially being or becoming infected, but are not experiencing physical symptoms. In these cases, there may or may not be a rational basis for their anxiety. These may seek health care partly as a preventive measure or due to their uncertainty as to risk. The third category consists of those who experience psychological distress during or after a traumatic event, such as chronic anxiety, depression, fatigue, and despair. These categories may overlap, but all represent unique problems that must be addressed in planning undertaken by disaster response teams and health facilities (p.8).

Disaster Mental Health Responsibilities

Many protocols for dealing with bioterrorism and pandemics recognize that mental health (sometimes referred to as behavioral health) professionals have an important role to play. Unfortunately, most of those plans don't go far beyond recognizing the roles and some of the tasks of mental health workers but fail to provide much detail regarding their training or treatment protocols.

In its 2004 *National Bioterrorism Hospital Preparedness Program*, the HRSA outlines ten critical benchmarks for surge capacity preparation: beds, isolation capacity, health care personnel, pharmaceutical caches, personal protective equipment, behavioral health, advanced registration, trauma and burn care, communication and information technology, and decontamination.

Advanced registration is defined as a plan to identify volunteers in the community who will be available to reinforce the existing medical staff during a surge in demand. It states, "Initial efforts should be directed toward identification of volunteer Physicians, Registered Nurses and Behavioral Health Professionals (including social workers, psychologists, psychiatrists, and therapists)." (Health Resources and Services Administration, p.14)

The national hospital preparedness program's surge capacity benchmark for Behavioral Health stipulates that the following points should be included in every plan:

> Enhance the networking capacity and training of health care professionals to be able to recognize, treat and coordinate care related to the behavioral health consequences of bioterrorism or other public health emergencies.
>
> ...develop behavioral health components of hospital preparedness plans that are integrated with other existing emergency behavioral health plans developed by the State behavioral health authority. These plans should include the following issues:

- behavioral health issues related to quarantine;
- behavioral health issues related to evacuation;
- addressing anxiety among patients and families;
- addressing need of patients with medically unexplained physical symptoms;
- family support in hospital settings;
- death notification;
- risk communication in coordination with public health authorities to educate the public on potential risks and whether they should report to hospitals. (p.21)

Triage

Any time conditions exist which cause more people to seek medical assistance than is available, choices must be made regarding who will receive treatment and who will have to wait. This is true when the first paramedics arrive at a multi-injury motor vehicle accident and on busy weekend evenings in emergency rooms. Medical personnel sort, screen and prioritize patients based on who is in greatest need. This selection process is called triage. In cases of mass casualties when there are limited resources, it is sometimes necessary to also include survivability into the triage equation. Difficult decisions must sometimes be made to allocate resources to those who are most likely to survive at the expense of those who are least likely.

Woodson (2006a) describes protocols for medical triage during pandemic influenza outbreaks that are adaptable to some types of bioterrorism agents as well. He uses the 1918 worldwide Spanish flu pandemic as a model for what can be expected if the H5N1 Avian Influenza or "bird flu" mutates so that it is easily transmitted from one human to another. As with most triage plans, he starts with the assumption that individuals presenting at hospitals have actually contracted the disease and describes procedures for treatment depending on the seriousness of the symptoms or likelihood of the patient's recovery.

Frederick "Skip" Burkel is the director of the Asia-Pacific Center for Biosecurity, Disaster and Conflict Research at the University of Hawaii John Burns Medical School (http://apitmid.hawaii.edu/APCBDCR.htm). He has written extensively about medical triage following disasters and recommended specific protocols which clinicians should use to make treatment decisions following bioterrorism attacks or during pandemics (Burkle, 2002, Burkle 2003, Burkle, 2006). He recognized that a significant resource consuming aspect of triage is dealing with the "worried well".

> Perhaps most difficulty will come in distinguishing those individuals actually exposed from those individuals potentially exposed, psychologically impaired casualties, individuals with multiple unexplained physical symptoms (MUPS), and those simply susceptible but concerned that they might have been exposed. This subgroup may well make up most of those seeking care. Triage personnel not accustomed to managing people with anxiety may under-triage these victims as "worried well." System planning must provide pre-designated programs for evaluation, education, and reassurance; emotional support can occur separate from but close to any health facility, to ensure ready access, availability, and compliance (p.424).

Disaster Mental Health Role

When exposed to traumatic or catastrophic events, people exhibit a wide range of emotional responses. Most people have an inherent natural resilience and develop useful mechanisms to cope with the stresses that accompany such experiences. Mental health professionals have observed and studied these reactions. A number of modalities (some controversial) have been developed to assist people who struggle to deal with emotional stresses in the wake of catastrophes.

Most of these interventions propose to offer "psychological first aid" to victims of disasters or other traumatic stress. Together, the various paradigms fall into a practice field called Disaster Mental Health. Some Disaster Mental Health interventions are provided informally by peers in workplace environments and some more closely resemble formal psychotherapy sessions. While many of those who provide Disaster Mental Health services in the wake of disasters are licensed professional psychiatrists, psychologists, marriage and family therapists, counselors, social workers or psychiatric nurses, the services may often more accurately be described as psychoeducational rather than psychotherapeutic.

This purpose of this paper is not to compare or contrast various paradigms of Disaster Mental Health. Instead, it proposes that the professionals who provide these services are a potential reservoir of talent that should be accessed by the medical community in order expand its surge capacity in the event of a bioterrorism attack or pandemic.

The Role of DMH in Pandemic and Bioterrorism Responses

While public health publications repeatedly recognize the potential for including behavioral health professionals in both hospital and regional response plans to pandemics or bioterrorism, there are few suggestions provided on how these suggestions can be implemented.

Even though the role to be played by Disaster Mental Health specialists is not always clear, researchers have recognized too few are available to meet potential needs. The Working Group on "Governance Dilemmas" in Bioterrorism Attacks found "few trained disaster mental health professionals, a weak infrastructure for implementing broad mental health protections, little knowledge on effective treatment, and scarce funds for long-term mental health care inhibit U.S. response to terrorism's psychological effects." Butler, Panzer, and Goldfrank, L.R. (2003) detail the need for greater disaster mental health capacity in order for the public health system to appropriately respond to terrorism.

Disaster Mental Health professionals are an obvious choice to assist family members of the ill or infected to deal with the stresses of their situations. They can also play a valuable role by assisting emergency services and medical facility employees deal with the emotional challenges presented when these staff members work in an infectious environment while worrying about their own loved ones being at risk of infection.

In recent workshops, Frederick "Skip" Burkel has described how Disaster Mental Health professionals are uniquely qualified to assist the medical community meet the threat of insufficient surge capacity presented by either a pandemic or bioterrorism attack. First, they have professional backgrounds in making differential psychiatric diagnoses that with proper training is transferable to the certain tasks required of a medical triage team. They understand the purposes and processes of diagnosis. His proposal in no way suggests that social workers, psychologists or marriage and family therapists without medical degrees are to be expected to make medical diagnoses and determine who is ill and who is not. It does propose that these mental health professionals can be trained to assist with non-symptom related triage activities such as determining whether the individual was likely to have been exposed to the disease or infective agent.

Second, Disaster Mental Health professionals have the professional training to help those who are not symptomatic and not likely to have been exposed deal with the anxiety they are experiencing. They should be equipped with communication skills that will allow them to redirect the "worried well" away from medical facilities and provide salient information on how individuals can further protect themselves from exposure or obtain available prophylactic treatment.

In Hawaii and elsewhere, Burkle has conducted workshops to teach mental health professionals basic triage skills that will enable them to work with and support the existing health services during a pandemic or following a bioterrorism attack. The multi-day seminars provide details of the medical, social and psychological impacts of such events and define ways in which mental health professionals can relieve some of the duties that would otherwise need to be carried out by medical staff. He does not propose that counselors or social workers will make medical diagnoses. Rather, their primary role would be to provide information to individuals regarding the likelihood that they have been infected, symptoms they should watch for and ways they can protect themselves from infection.

The mental health professionals would work in a number of different environments including hospitals, telephone hotlines and triage centers. Their primary focus would be on relieving medical professionals from the responsibility of dealing with the worried-well.

Burkel recognizes that there is a great deal of work that must be done to clearly establish ways to organize, train and supervise these efforts. In some areas, local chapters of the American Red Cross have taken the lead in organizing training classes and bringing together representatives of the many different organizations and agencies that will need to work together during a pandemic or following a bioterrorism attack.

One concern voiced by several experienced disaster mental health workers regards liability insurance. Medical triage probably does not fall into the generally recognized scope of practice for most mental health professionals. Some have expressed reluctance to become involved in a program such as this unless there is an umbrella sponsoring agency that can offer liability coverage similar to that offered by the American Red Cross to Disaster Mental Health volunteers.

Conclusion

The American health care system does not have sufficient surge capacity to deal with a major pandemic or bioterrorism attack. While there is a general philosophical recognition of those deficiencies, the task of building a system that will be able to respond is overwhelming. This paper proposes one possibility for adding additional capacity that may be able to help deal with the panic and crush of the "worried-well" during one of these eventualities.

Until all of the players in the response system and the citizens for whom they are responsible recognize the dire straits in which they will find themselves during one of the events described in this paper, there is little hope the significant resources required to prepare a response will be forthcoming. If such preparation is postponed much longer, a catastrophe that could eclipse the unnecessary consequences of September 11 and Hurricane Katrina may result.

About the Author

Thom Curtis, Ph.D., is an Associate Professor at the University of Hawaii at Hilo where he focuses on terrorism and disaster psychology/sociology. He has participated in numerous disaster responses from Guam to New York and served as a consultant to government and private agencies involved in disasters. Over the two years, he has traveled across the Atlantic three times to conduct terrorism related research in Europe, the Middle East and North Africa. While his primary focus is on the social and psychological attributes of terrorists, he has also examined the resiliency of direct and indirect survivors of terrorism attacks in Israel, Europe and the U.S. His recent work includes journal articles titled, "Child Abuse in the Wake of Natural Disasters" and "Fatal Aviation Accidents in Rural Communities: Response Preparation Strategies and presentations titled "The Path to Jihad: Recruitment of U.S. Citizens by Islamist Organizations" and "Native Hawaiian Perceptions of Violence as a Means to Attain Sovereignty". He also edited the book, *Hawaii Remembers September 11*. He is a licensed Marriage and Family Therapist and American Red Cross Disaster Mental Health Instructor.

To discuss or obtain a copy of this paper, please contact:

Thom Curtis, Ph.D.
Department of Sociology
University of Hawaii-Hilo
200 West Kawili Street
Hilo, Hawaii 96720

thomc@hawaii.edu

References

Agency for Healthcare Research and Quality. (2006). *Addressing Surge Capacity in a Mass Casualty Event Issue Brief #9*. Washington, DC: US Department of Health and Human Services, Public Health Service. Last accessed November 2, 2006: http://www.ahrq.gov/news/ulp/btbriefs/btbrief9.pdf

Agency for Healthcare Research and Quality. (2004). *Optimizing Surge Capacity: Hospital Assessment and Planning*. Washington, DC: US Department of Health and Human Services, Public Health Service. Last accessed October 22, 2006: http://www.ahrq.gov/news/ulp/btbriefs/btbrief3.pdf

American Hospital Association. (2005). *Fast Facts on US Hospitals*. Last accessed October 22, 2006: http://www.aha.org/aha/resource-center/Statistics-and-Studies/fast-facts.html

Beaton, R., Stergachis, A., Oberle, M., Bridges, E., Nemuth, M. and Thomas, T. (2005). The sarin gas attacks of the Tokyo subway – 10 years later/Lessons learned. *Traumatology*, 11 (2) pp. 103-119.

Bogdan, G.M. (2004) *Addressing Surge Capacity through Information Exchange*. Research Presentation at Colorado's Health Emergency Line for the Public Web Conference. Last accessed October 22, 2006: http://www.ahrq.gov/news/ulp/btsurgemass/bogdantxt.htm

Burkle. F.M. (200) Population-based triage management in response to surge-capacity requirements during a large-scale bioevent disaster

Burkle. F.M. (2003) Measures of effectiveness in large-scale bioterrorism events. *Prehospital and Disaster Medicine*, 18 (3); 258-262.

Burkle. F.M. (2002) Mass casualty management of a large-scale bioterrorist event: An epidemiological approach that shapes triage decisions. *Emergency Medical Clinics of North America*, 20, 409-436

Butler, A.S., Panzer, A.M., Goldfrank, L.R. (2003). *Preparing for the psychological consequences of terrorism: A public health strategy*. Washington, DC: Institutes of Medicine.

Health Resources and Services Administration. (2004). *National Bioterrorism Hospital Preparedness Program*. Washington, DC: US Department of Health and Human Services. Last accessed October 22, 2006: http://www.dhs.ca.gov/epo/PDF/HRSAbhppguidance.pdf

Inglesby, T.V., Nuzzo, J.B., O'Toole, T, & Henderson, D.A. (2006). Disease mitigation measures in the control of pandemic influenza. *Biosecurity and Bioterrorism: Biodefense Strategy, Practice and Science* 4 (4)

Kaydos-Daniels, S.C., Olowokure, B., Chang, H., Barwick, R.S., Deng, J., Lee, Kuo, S.H., Su, I., Chen, & K. Maloney, S.A. (2004). Body temperature monitoring and SARS fever hotline, Taiwan. *Emerging Infectious Diseases* 10 (2) pp. 373-376 Last accessed October 22, 2006: http://www.cdc.gov/ncidod/Eid/vol10no2/pdfs/03-0748.pdf

Lurie, N., Valdez, R. B., Wasserman, J., Stoto, M., Myers, S., Molander, R., Asch, S., Mussington, B.D., & Solomon, M. (2004). *Public health preparedness in*

California: Lessons learned from seven health jurisdictions. Santa Monica, CA: The RAND Corporation. Last accessed October 22, 2006: http://www.rand.org/pubs/technical_reports/2005/RAND_TR181.pdf

Morgan, J. (1994). Providing Disaster Mental Health Services Through The American Red Cross. *NCP Clinical Quarterly* 4(2) Last accessed October 30, 2006: http://www.ncptsd.va.gov/publications/cq/v4/n2/morgan.html

Nevada Health Association. (2006). *Disaster medical response: A model for America.* Last accessed November 2, 2006: http://www.nvha.net/bio/postings/2006surgecapq1.pdf

Olson, K.B. (1999). Aum Shinrikyo: Once and future threat? *Emerging and Infectious Diseases,* 5 (4) pp. 513-516.

Pilch, F. (2003) The worried well: Strategies for installation commanders. Colorado Springs, CO: United States Air Force Accademy. www.usafa.af.mil/inss/OCP/OCP53.pdf

Seeman, B.T. (July 20, 2005) U.S. *Ill-Prepared for Flu Pandemic, Experts Fear.* Newhouse News Service. Last accessed October 22, 2006 http://www.newhousenews.com/archive/seeman072005.html

Taneda, K. (2005). The sarin gas attack on the Tokyo subway: Hospital responses to mass casualties and psychological issues in hospital planning. *Traumatology,* 11 (2) pp. 75-85.

Woodson, G. (2006a). Patient triage during a pandemic. *The Bird Flu Manaual.com.* Last accessed November 2, 2006: http://www.birdflumanual.com/articles/patTriage.asp

Woodson, G. (2006b). Pandemic disruption of essential services and supplies. *The Bird Flu Manaual.com.* Last accessed November 2, 2006: http://www.birdflumanual.com/articles/panDisrupt.asp

Appendix A – Glossary of Disease Mitigation Measures

The following definitions are from "Disease Mitigation Measures in the Control of Pandemic Influenza" published in Biosecurity and Bioterrorism: *Biodefense Strategy, Practice and Science* Volume 4, Number 4, 2006

By Thomas V. Inglesby, Jennifer B. Nuzzo, Tara O'Toole, and D. A. Henderson.

CLARIFICATION OF TERMS

There is widespread confusion about the terms used to describe measures for controlling disease spread. The principal confusion is between use of the words *quarantine* and *isolation*.

Isolation properly refers only to the confinement of *symptomatic* patients in the hospital (or at home) so that they will not infect others.

Quarantine has traditionally been defined as the separation from circulation in the community of *asymptomatic* people who may have been exposed to infection and might—or might not—become ill.

Home quarantine refers to voluntary confinement of known contacts of influenza cases in their own homes.

Large-scale quarantine typically refers to confinement of large groups of possibly infected people—for example, all passengers on an airplane, or the residents of an apartment building or an entire city—for periods of days to weeks.

In recent years, the term *social distancing* has come into use. *Social distancing* has been used to refer to a range of measures that might serve to reduce contact between people. These may include closing schools or prohibiting large gatherings, such as church services and sporting events. Others have used the term to refer to actions taken to increase the distance of individuals from each other at the work site or in other locations—for example, substituting phone calls for face-to-face meetings or avoiding handshaking. The term has come to describe fundamentally different approaches to disease mitigation.

Care for the Caretaker

Patricia Justice, BACP Fellow

Abstract

This article is for those people involved in disaster work of any description whether they be psychiatrists, counsellors, fireman, policeman, hospital workers, receptions, health workers in related fields and even those who make the coffee, on lookers who are either related to or through unfortunate circumstances watched the catastrophe. How, why, where and when should we be taking care of ourselves?

This subject was brought home to me personally after being personally involved in a terrorist bomb attack in the east end of London, England on February 9, 1996. Due to my specialty as a trauma therapist, I was called in to debrief workers and locals who had been affected by the massive blast. This was in the early days of trauma work for survivors and workers and as I was working freelance, there was nothing set up for our own debriefing. After working practically non-stop for 36 hours and weeks afterwards on top of my normal workload I recognize now that I became quite hyperactive and didn't stop working. At the time, I was also doing a masters degree in applied psychoanalytic theory and changed my whole dissertation to look at the effects on the counselors who had been involved in the work after the bombing. This was an excellent way for me to work through my own personal thoughts and collated information from the counselors whom I managed to track down after much difficulty during the following months.

What it is that makes us think we are invincible and just take events on the chin? Is it fear of looking soft and weak, fear of losing one's job if you talk about your own personal responses and feelings? Is it being strong for everyone else in a neighborhood or team? There are as many questions as answers. However, until this debate was opened little was discussed about the workers' emotional states. We know very well now that we can also suffer secondary traumatization and show signs and symptoms very similar to the people actually involved.

It makes sense that after working through many of these events, one does not necessarily get better at coping with it. It is more likely that the human psyche can only take so much. This depends on one's own personal situation at the time with work, family, commitments and friendships. Disasters never happen at a convenient time and the more stressed and worn out we are the harder it can be to cope.

I was affected personally by the Tsunami of 2004 where I voluntarily went out to both Sri Lanka and Thailand one month afterwards. I have never seen such devastation or worked with people who had literally lost everything.

Life had never been brilliant for many of those people but now, overnight, it became a thousand times worse. In addition, the very able and capable workers, who rushed to help, became more than overloaded. Can you imagine seeing hundreds of bodies wrapped in white sheets lying out on the road, outside hospitals and temples just waiting for identification? The smell was the worst sense to be assaulted as, in the heat, bodies soon began to deteriorate.

The refrigerated trucks were full and DNA testing was still taking place in 2006 when I re-visited Thailand for the fifth time. Workers were emotionally and physically drained, but who was to take their place. Could you drain ditches to find bodies, or walk in the sea amidst float-ing corpses, broken buildings, wires and pieces of peoples' clothing, be asked everyday if you had seen so and so, looked at thousands of pictures of people who were lost or missing? The whole area was full of grieving relatives and friends of not only Thais, but also the myriad of nationalities that were on holiday in these luxurious idyllic spots.

The fact that it was Christmas as well, made it even more poignant. The amount of money raised worldwide was astronomical as it affected the majority of the world in one way or other. In London, where I live, locals still talk about it as quite a few people from this small area died, including a well-known music teacher from a local school. Many had relatives who were in the area at the time and memorial services are still taking place two years later to commemo-rate the event lest we forget.

In April 2006, I was in Thailand for the fifth time, following up survivors I had worked with and teaching the Thais EMDR therapy, which they were finding very useful in their work not only with survivors but also in hospital units etc where they worked. In addition, the helpers who just really didn't know what to do or say acquired basic counseling skills. With very little equipment, they had to improvise and just help in whatever way they could.

I was in involved in a near fatal car accident on Songkrat which is Thai New Year and this year fell on Maunday Thursday. I rolled over a cliff 15 times and landed up in a stagnant lake. My partner managed to break the windows and get me out of the car. He then struggled to lift me on the roof and gave me mouth-to-mouth resuscitation. I was unconscious and under water 3-4 minutes. He had lost his wife and baby son through drowning because of the tsunami. For him this was like a re-run of the event and equally traumatizing, as he had found his son 3 days later in the debris and as he lifted him up his flesh fell away in his hands. I had broken both arms, fractured my right ankle, had a collapsed left lung and a brain hemorrhage. He spent most of the 4 days I was unconscious in ICU on his knees praying for my survival. No-body thought I would recover and if I did, I would most certainly be brain damaged. But I proved them wrong!

I entered the world of the living again on Easter Sunday like a resurrection. Although hav-ing to spend the next 3 weeks in a Thai hospital wrapped in a sheet (all of my belongings were either lost or stolen) I certainly had my mind with me even though looking like I had just had 10 rounds in a boxing ring. I was eventually flown back to the UK and landed back in hospital in London as my right arm needed re-fixing and now has a huge metal plate in it. This causes havoc with the metal detectors at the airports. However, within 3 months I managed to carry on working and have enormous gratitude not only to my man Glen but also to the many tsu-nami survivors who traveled long distances to visit me in hospital.

Whilst visiting in August 2005 with my two daughters, they persuaded me to informally "adopt" two girls who had lost everything including their parents due to the tsunami. The younger of the two called Khoa Mook, had on reflection and from past photographs, adopted me! The older sister appropriately nicknamed Joy, happened to be a chef and she visited every day in hospital and washed and fed me. Originally when I gave her a lot of money she was overwhelmed and commented that "When you come back Thailand we do everything for you and look after you as you are now our mommy".

Now, one can say it was a fluke accident, or was it as a result of the overload or work I had taken on continually following my tsunami work. I had also visited Sri Lanka twice and taken a family for a short holiday after they had repaired their home 18 months later.

In my 22 years as a psychotherapist (10 years as a trauma specialist), I had always managed to keep my personal and work life separate. The previous summer my two daughters returned with me and worked voluntarily in schools teaching English, sponsored a child, made a video of our work and brought back many of the handicraft goods made by the survivors in order to raise money for them by selling their handicrafts in local London markets. My son also visited with his new fiancé in February 2006 to see how he could help. I divorced my husband of 37 years at the beginning of the year and 2 months later, I met the man who saved my life. He was suffering from PTSD because of the tsunami. The huge impact it has had on my life is obvious, yet I was sitting comfortably enjoying Christmas in London on the day it happened.

As I work on a freelance voluntary basis with this work, I had not really had anyone to work it through with or someone who would understand the circumstances and the sheer enormity of the event. We did have an informal support network whilst in Thailand for one month during our work together following the tsunami. We would try to relax in the evenings and debrief each other but working 12 hours or more most days we were all overloaded. I was the only person from the charity called Making Waves that came from England, not forgetting that my primary role had been to debrief the workers involved. However, who was there to look after me?

I do recall that I had a desperate need to call my children back home. I needed some sort of reality being connected to a normal place, with a normal life going on elsewhere when all around was just chaos. I worked hard and well and helped over 206 people recover and have now many new friends both Thai and various nationalities, but there has been a price to pay for my family. All our lives have changed because of it.

Whilst researching my dissertation on *Care for the Caretaker* I came across quite a few incidents where workers had divorced, separated and had big life changes since the disaster they had worked with. These facts are rarely reported, as obviously we are more concerned about the actual victims and survivors, but the exact number of workers' lives that are affected as well is a considerable proportion of those responding.

Naturally, we are individuals, as are the survivors of disasters, but how we manage is a very personal thing and it is imperative that we consider our own mental health. Failing to do this may cause havoc with those who go to help and a great loss of those individuals whose experience and knowledge is so valuable to all.

Take a moment or two right now to think of what you might need or what you could do to take care of yourself. Whom you could talk to? Not just friends and family who soon are overloaded too and may not be the support you need for your own recovery.

At the conference, which turned out to be one of the better ones in the honesty of attendees and presenters expressing their thoughts, emotions and vulnerabilities, the majority saw that we couldn't be superheroes. This was a huge learning curve for many, regardless of their position or cultural background.

During the last of the sessions, we discussed the subject area of Katrina and race and culture and how this may or may not differ. The importance of cross-cultural work was being highlighted. An appreciation and understanding of where others are coming from, showing respect for every individual is important. Failing this, it is possible to leave them further traumatized and it would have been better if we had left some people well alone.

I do a lot of cross cultural teaching and work and believe London and other parts of Europe are much more aware than parts of America. This could be because we are much older and have always had immigrants coming to our lands. I met an American Indian, a social worker from the Northern Arapaho Tribe (Tribal Liaison to the Wyoming Governor's Office) and four black people (two of whom are academic doctors who had worked with victims of Katrina relocated to Philadelphia, PA) who gave a presentation of their work following the disaster in New Orleans. This distressed me as I would have liked to have seen more cross-cultural awareness. America could learn from some of the examples of its neighbors across the pond.

However, the conference had a very positive ending as one of my strengths is getting people talking and communicating together, and in the last workshop a seed was sown. It only takes one person to set off an avalanche and a long journey starts with a single step.

Don't be afraid to speak up, show your vulnerability, look for support and help if needed and most of all look after yourself. You will then do your job of helping others involved in such huge life events in a far more productive way and help their recovery too. Like a stone in a pond, it all has ripple effects. Believe me I have witnessed it.

About the Author

Patricia Justice runs the Docklands Counselling & Psychotherapy Services in the East End of London and works with many EAP's (Employment Assistance Programmes) and trains Government Health & Safety Inspectors in dealing with major incidents. She is a supervisor and also teaches on various counseling related courses. As Vice Chair of the Personal Relationship & Group Work Division of the British Association of Counselling & Psychotherapy this division represents Practioners in Private Practice. Involved both personally and professionally following the I.R.A. Docklands Bomb in 1996 she then specialized in working with traumatized individuals and bereaved families. This involved her in many UK and International critical incidents. Previous papers published relate to these and her experience with diverse cultures, gives her a unique perspective for her ongoing work, currently with Tsunami survivors and in the very recent London bombings.

International Critical Incident Stress Foundation Online Learning Project

Richard J. Conroy, MS, Assistant Chief (ret.)

Abstract

The International Critical Incident Stress Foundation (ICISF), in partnership with Weber State University is pleased to announce an on-line learning initiative that will help broaden the availability of updated training material to those involved in the Crisis Intervention, Peer Support, and disaster mental health fields.

Background

Weber State University received grant funding to explore the expansion of critical incident stress management training in the Western US. One of the grant objectives was to help make training information available to students in new and innovative ways.

As the primary source for information and training about Critical Incident Stress Management (CISM), historically the ICISF has conducted regional conferences all over the country. Faculty have come from a diverse group of approximately 750 trained trainers who have completed ICISF trained trainer courses over many years. In an effort to keep those who train on behalf of the ICISF, as well as those who have taken ICISF training previously, up to date on issues, trends and changes in the field, the online learning project was initiated.

The pilot course developed for online access is titled *The Changing Face of Crisis and Disaster Mental Health Intervention.* The content expert for this course on behalf of the International Critical Incident Stress Foundation (ICISF) was George S. Everly, Jr., PhD, FAPM, CTS, ICISF's Chairman of the Board Emeritus and Representative to the United Nations. He is co-founder of the International Critical Incident Stress Foundation, Inc. and is on the faculty of Loyola College in Maryland.

Course Objective

The overall purpose of this course is to provide an ongoing update in the fields of critical incident response, crisis intervention, and disaster mental health. These fields are in constant flux, evolving with every major disaster. Every week the headlines reflect terrorism, natural disasters, and fears of pandemics. New information comes out regularly. It is therefore necessary to keep those who must meet these challenges abreast of important changes as they occur. These updates can be an important medium to provide access to the latest trends, theories, research and practice.

The course consists of six learning modules:
- Terms and Definitions
- The Nature of Crisis Reactions
- Empirical Foundations of Crisis Intervention, Critical Incident Stress Management and Disaster Mental Health
- Introduction to Strategic and Tactical Planning
- Increasing Intervention Effectiveness & Reducing the Risk of Harm

- Innovations and Recent Trends in Crisis Intervention and Disaster Mental Health

The course includes directed student learning activities, video and movie clip links, journal article access and quizzes. To successfully complete the course, students will be required to pass each of the quizzes with a score of 80% or higher.

Access to the course will be through Weber State University's online learning system. Students will register for the non-credit course through Continuing Education at Weber State. There will be a small fee for the class and Continuing Education units will be offered from Weber State University.

Mandatory Update Requirement (Effective Date to be Determined)

1. In order for current and future ICISF trained trainers to maintain their trainer certification, they will be <u>required</u> to complete the "update" course every two to three years.
2. In order for current and future holders of a Certificate of Specialized Training from ICISF to maintain this certificate, they will be <u>required</u> to complete the "update" course every three years.
3. Current CISM teams registered with ICISF will also be <u>encouraged</u> to have their team clinical director and/or team coordinator complete the "update" course every two years, as part of their team's continuing education.

These mandatory update requirements will serve to develop consistency in the body of knowledge shared by those practicing and teaching disaster mental health and crisis intervention programs. It is envisioned that students will be able to print their own completion certificate, after completing the course requirements. Weber State University will report enrollment and completion information back to the ICISF.

Anticipated Development Timeline

January 1-15, 2007	Identify five (5) ICISF current trainers to review course content as peer reviewers.
January 15-30, 2007	Make content and curriculum changes to course, based on initial peer review.
February 1 – 28, 2007-	Beta test course by 25 ICISF current trainers.
March 1 – 30, 2007 -	Make content and curriculum changes to course based on beta test review.
April 1, 2007	Public course release via WSU Web CT.

About the Author

Richard J. Conroy, MSCJ is a program administrator and co-principal investigator of a CISM grant project at Weber State University. He retired from law enforcement, having served as an Assistant Chief of Police at the municipal level. He is a life member of the International Association of Chiefs of Police and was a co-coordinator in the late 1980's of a Florida multi-disciplinary CISM team. Mr. Conroy has published in the FBI Law Enforcement Bulletin on CISM. He served as a police academy faculty member and developed a recruit level, role-playing training curriculum in crisis intervention. Mr. Conroy holds a Certificate in Specialized Training (Emergency Services) from the International Critical Incident Stress Foundation and is a member of the program planning committee for the 9th World Congress on Stress, Trauma and Coping, to be held in Baltimore, MD in February 2007.

Preparing Communities for Deployment and Return of Military Members and Their Families

Debra Russell, Family Assistance Center Supervisor
Wyoming National Guard and Reserve

Many community members are not familiar with the military and what they do. Community members consist of various agencies, organizations, employers, co-workers, family and friends.

Because of the numerous deployments, Family Assistance Centers (FACs) were opened to work with family members of those that are deployed helping them through this difficult time. The phases the FACs work with the families are Deployment, Sustainment, and Reunion. We want to ensure that we leave no family member or friend behind. In addition to working with the family member and the service member of those deployed, we also provide services to the Veterans and Retirees. The Family Assistance Centers are 24/7 and work with all services and all components.

During the Deployment phase, we work to build a bond with the families so they feel comfortable sharing difficulties they may be encountering with us such as; financial issues, serious illness, injury or death. After continuing to stay in contact with the families for 18 months we develop a close relationship with them. We call each family member a minimum of once a month, send monthly newsletters, and offer one activity a month for them to attend. These activities give them the opportunity to meet other families that are going through the same situation as they are.

FACs support our Service Members and are dedicated to helping families help themselves and each other. We are here for them, to provide services to families, military members, our state, and our nation. FACs are vital to the welfare of our families during deployments. They are critical links for families, Service Members, commands and community. FACs are strategically placed in the state to overcome the geographic distance that frequently separates families from centralized, installation-based services. FACs are the primary entry point for assistance for all Service Members regardless of service or component and provide information, referral, and outreach to Service Members and families during the deployment process.

FACs are not just an indispensable pillar of support for families of deployed Service Members—they also provide critical assistance to demobilizing Service Members and promote the long-term health and welfare of the military family.

Family Assistance is composed of prescribed functions and services provided to military families by the military as a policy and regulatory requirement. FACs assist in identifying programs and services that provide many opportunities for personal growth and strengthening of Department of Defense (DOD) families. We take care of families at home and help family members handle their situations on the home front so the military member does not have to worry about their family. In turn, this helps the military member focus on their mission and keep it safe. FACs call families to find out how they are doing and what they may need. We keep in touch with families via emails and through the telephone.

We ensure accurate and timely information, one stop shopping with a "no run-around" rule. FACs work on being proactive not reactive! We provide information, referral, resources, and advocacy.

FACs also teach and mentor unit lead volunteers and their family support groups to help them provide additional assistance for families in need. We accompany casualty assistance officers if the need arises. FACs travel with spouses and other family members who may need to visit injured or ill military members or family members.

During the Sustainment phase of the deployment, we encourage spouses to go to school, work part time, start their own private business, become involved with volunteer work, or church involvement. This helps the family member to stay busy and helps with overcoming depression that they may be encountering.

During the Reunion phase of the deployment, we provide briefings that are critical to the health of our military members and their families. The scope of the briefs are to provide family members information of trends that some families tend to experience after they are re-united following a deployment to a combat theater of operations. The secondary mission is to ensure families have as much information as possible concerning resources available to help in the re-union process. The reunion phase tends to be more stressful than the deployment and separation.

The service member encounters trauma daily while they are in theater experiencing convoy attacks, continual live fire, and Improvised Explosive Devices, (IED's). Service members may suffer with PTSD symptoms after returning home.

After the military member returns, they are not required to drill for 90 days. At this time, they are provided with REFRAD (RElease FRom Active Duty) briefings to include Employer Support of the Guard and Reserve, (ESGR) TRICARE – UCCI Insurance, Vet Center, VA Hospital benefits, and Chaplain Services with One on One Support.

The family has grown and changed during this separation becoming self sufficient and independent in order to survive. However, they expect the military member to be the same as they were when they left 18 months ago. The military member has had major changes due to their experiences while in theater. However, they also tend to expect to find things at home to be just the same as they were when they left. To assist the family in adjusting we offer a PREP (Marriage Retreat Seminar) to help the family with communication and understanding of their relationship.

The families experience five phases of reunion; Pre-Entry Phase which is the first few days before actual reunion, fantasies, excitement, work, planning, and thoughts.

The Reunion Phase, which is the immediate, and the first few days after arrival include courtship, relearning, intimacy, a happy time, and the honeymoon period.

The Disruption Phase is when problems surface, independence, differences surface, routines get interrupted, financial problems, control, thoughts, trust, jealousy, hard times stories, decision making, unresolved problems/issues, and children issues.

The Communication Phase is a time of renegotiating new routines, reconnecting, redefining family roles, acceptance of control and decision-making. New rules will be established. Things to expect in this phase are: renegotiation, trust, reconnection, acceptance, and explanation of new rules.

The Normal Phase is when they get back to the normal family routine of sharing, growing, and experiencing the difficulties, happiness and sadness of a family. Things to expect in this phase are: establishment of routines, acceptance of change, and personal growth.

As community members some wonder what they can do to help with the adjustment back in their community. Be there for them, some may not want to talk. Let them have their space; don't try to force the service member to talk about their experience. At some time, ask them if they would like to talk then listen to them. Show a genuine concern about their experience whether they choose to share or not. Don't act as if the 1-½ years did not exist and don't criticize.

The FACs have many resources available for referral if needed to include Military One Source, Troop and Family Counseling, Chaplain Services, PREP Seminars, Vet Centers and the VA Hospitals.

About the Author

Debbie Russell is a Specialist with the Wyoming Family Program. She supervises and trains the Family Assistance Center Representatives and assists in training the Lead Volunteers. Debbie Russell began working with the Family Program in 1987 as a volunteer then accepted the position as the FAC Supervisor in 2003. Being a parent and spouse of a service member for 26 years she recognizes the need for providing assistance to families before, during and after deployment.

Summaries of Additional Presentations

The four-day Rocky Mountain Region Disaster Mental Health Conference in Casper, Wyoming in November 2006 included a large number of presentations, not all of which developed papers for publication. However, in an attempt to make these proceedings more complete, summaries of the remaining presentations are included below.

Pandemic Flu Update

Dr. Richard Luce,
Wyoming Department of Health

Pandemic Influenza is currently a major global public health concern and the focus of extensive ongoing planning efforts at the federal, state, and local level. This talk provided a basic review of the history and biology of influenza viruses, an update on the current avian influenza situation internationally, and provided information on preparation and planning efforts being conducted by the Wyoming Department of Health.

Understanding the Abnormal Grief Spiral of Human Response to an Abnormal Event OR How to Shake Off the Sucker Punch of Life

David Sones, RNCS, APN-BC
Cheyenne Veterans Medical Center

Over the years since Dr. Elisabeth Kubler-Ross (1996) first described the stages of loss, many pioneers in the mental health field have attempted to identify how each of these stages affect individuals or groups pathologically. Many, such as Jeffrey Mitchell, Ph.D. of the International Critical Incident Stress Foundation (ICISF), have attempted to use this knowledge as a means of preventing the long term effects of dysfunctional grief or sudden emotional trauma. However, the sequence and onset of these stages has long been felt to be unpredictable. Today, with improved understanding of the neuron-chemical responses, learned coping skills development, cognitive and behavioral concepts, we are now able to use the stages of grief to predict human response. Through this understanding, we are able to predict grief reactions to more positive/supportive interventions allowing for a rapid return to stability from the sucker punch of life. "Events which have sufficient emotional power to overwhelm a person's usual effective ability to cope." (Mitchell, 1995). Our ultimate goal is the re-establishment of predictability, which leads to a return to stability.

Fire on the Mountain: The Jackson Canyon Fire and The Family Assistance Center (FAC): More Than Coffee and Doughnuts

Stewart Anderson, Natrona County Emergency Management Coordinator and Theresa Simpson, Natrona County Deputy Emergency Management Coordinator

On Monday, August 14, 2006 Natrona County Emergency Management were called out for a wildfire on Casper Mountain. Their response involved coordinating the largest evacuation and sheltering in Wyoming. This presentation discussed the aspects of fighting the fire, the evacuation/sheltering and the toll it took on both evacuees and responders.

In a related presentation, Anderson and Simpson presented information about Family Assistance Centers (FAC). This presentation looked at planning a family assistance center from the finding and setting up of a facility to when to break it down. Setting up and running a center on a 24-hour basis as well as all of the services needed was discussed.

Response to Tornado in Wright, Wyoming

David King, Campbell County Emergency Manager and Leslie Flocchini

This presentation provided information concerning the response to the tornado that occurred in Wright, Wyoming on August 12, 2005 leading to a Presidential Disaster Declaration. The recovery efforts are still ongoing for some Wright residents. However, much of the community has resumed a normal routine. David King oversaw the Emergency Operations Center in the days and weeks that followed the tornado's impact. Leslie Flocchini has been one of the leaders in working with Wright residents in the aftermath and recovery of the community.

A Soldier's Trauma: Everyone's Trauma

Nancy L. Day, CTS, CTM

Trauma is a personal relationship with an experience. For a soldier and a soldier's family, trauma may occur during mobilization, deployment, employment, re-deployment and/or demobilization. The ripple effect of a soldier's trauma can affect us all. Traumatic Incident Reduction (TIR) provides a tool to do something about it by going to the root of the trauma. This presentation discussed a method, (TIR), designed to permanently resolve PTSD quickly, privately and without negative side effects.

Wind River All Hazards Team

Allison Sage, MSW
Northern Arapaho Tribe

This presentation provided information about the ongoing development process of constructing an All Hazards Emergency Preparedness System for the Wind River Indian Reservation. The Wind River Indian Reservation has two tribes living on it and consists of 2.2 million acres. The population of the enrolled members of both tribes and the residents of Fremont County is close to 34,000. The presentation discussed the collaboration of a multitude of governments, departments, and agencies and explained the different authorities involved. One important aspect of implementing this emergency preparedness system is education and mobilizing the residents of the Wind River Indian Reservation due to cultural awareness factors. The delegates to the conference learned and developed a better understanding of the challenges involved in implementing an emergency response system within an Indian reservation and with other governmental agencies.

Preparing for the Worst: Pre-disaster Emotional Hardiness for Clinical and Administrative Staff

Melinda D. Koenig, Psy.D.
St. Luke's Roosevelt Hospital, New York, NY

In the event of a disaster, psychological victims are expected to outnumber medical victims by as many as ten times or more. A disaster can be expected to affect healthcare professionals in immediate and prolonged ways that may impair their ability to care for disaster victims. Healthcare professionals experience the same risk factors as the population in general, but are called upon to respond regardless of their personal risk. The community in which one works has a great deal of influence over workers' ability to withstand either acute or chronic stress. By addressing predictable stressors, anticipating possible pathological reaction, and by increasing staff resilience, the healthcare facility can improve disaster response. By simple training in psychological first aid staff can have response tools on hand to address the anticipated psychological demands of individuals affected by disaster or severe emergencies. Staff who understand normal reactions, who are aware of their own vulnerabilities, and who know how to respond are more able to withstand the impact of acute stress on themselves. This presentation addressed pre-disaster emotional preparedness for healthcare staff from the viewpoint of current literature, from Meichenbaum's ideas of "stress inoculation", from Crimando's techniques for "psychological first aid", as well as from issues in corporate hardiness.

Disaster and Triage: Implications for Mental Health Professionals

Norman Linzer, PhD; Heidi Heft La Porte, MSW; and Jay Sweifach, MSW, DSW.
Wurzweiler School of Social Work, Yeshiva University

Social workers are among the key allied professionals who provide vital care during emergency situations; they are expected to provide services while concomitantly sorting out personal reactions, and other challenges caused by the disaster. During these moments, choices about service provision with ethical implications are numerous. This presentation highlighted the results of an international qualitative study examining the impact of terrorism on social work agencies and their labor force. The study was conducted with focus groups of social workers in health care and social service settings. The major research question concerned the impact of disasters on agencies and social work practitioners. Focus was placed on the ethical dissonance experienced by social workers as a result of triage-based decisions that needed to be made.

About the Authors

Allison Sage, MSW, is an enrolled member of the Northern Arapaho Tribe and is currently serving as the Tribal Liaison for the Governor of the State of Wyoming to the Northern Arapaho Tribal Council. Allison has experience in being a past Northern Arapaho Tribal Council member for the term of 2002-2004. He has worked as an Administrator for the Northern Arapaho Department of Social Services which administers the Northern Arapaho Temporary Assistance to Needy Families and the Child Protection Services programs. Presently Allison teaches an Introduction to Social Work class at the Wind River Tribal College in Ethete, WY.

Theresa Simpson started her public safety career working as a controller in the Laramie County Jail. She served in this capacity for two years before leaving and becoming a stay-at-home-mom. In 2000, Theresa was employed with the City of Casper as a Public Safety Communications Specialist. In June of 2002, she joined the Natrona County Sheriff's Office serving in the Emergency Management Division. Theresa is currently serving her community as the Natrona County Deputy Emergency Management Coordinator. In this position, she serves as acting Emergency Management Coordinator, is the lead in Project Lifesaver, assists in administering and instructing the Community Emergency Response Team (CERT) program and trains various other agencies, responders and citizens in topics such as the Incident Command System, Disaster Preparedness, CPR, Basic Emergency Care, Emergency Planning and various other response and preparedness classes. She also assists in all phases of Emergency Management; Mitigation, Preparedness, Response and Recovery. Theresa is married with 4 children and enjoys spending her precious little off-duty time with her family.

David E. Sones, RNCS,APRN, BC received his Master's Degree in Psychology from Norwich University of Vermont, his Bachelors in Nursing from the University of Wisconsin and a Bachelors in Health Science from George Washington University. He received additional training as an Independent Duty Hospital Corpsman with the U.S. Navy, Emergency Medical Technician, Alcohol and Drug Counselor (Wisconsin), PTSD Counselor (Wyoming), Grief Counselor (Wyoming), Critical Incident Counselor with Red Cross (Wyoming), Critical Incident Counselor with Wyoming Assist Program, Mass Fatalities Incident Response Training, and is an educator for Disruptive Behavioral Management. He is currently employed with Mental Health Services of the Cheyenne Veterans Medical Center.

Jay Sweifach (jsweifac@yu.edu) - Assistant Professor, Wurzweiler School of Social Work, Yeshiva University Areas of Expertise: Domestic violence, Jewish communal service, groupwork education, use of information technology, HIV education Degrees: MSW, DSW, Wurzweiler School of Social Work, Yeshiva University.

Norman Linzer Areas of Expertise: Jewish community, professional values and ethics Degrees: MSW, Yeshiva University; MA, PhD, New School University; Ordination, Rabbi Isaac Elchanan Theological Seminary.

Dr. Richard Luce is a veterinarian with the U.S. Centers for Disease Control and Prevention's Epidemic Intelligence Service. He is currently assigned to the Wyoming Department of Health. His work on issues of importance to public health includes avian influenza at the state planning level as well as internationally with the CDC avian influenza field team in Nigeria. He earned his veterinary degree from North Carolina State University's College of Veterinary Medicine and has practiced large animal medicine in Texas. He also earned a Master's degree in Veterinary Science and Epidemiology from the University of Cambridge.

David Allen King is the coordinator for the Campbell County Emergency Management Agency,. David is a past President of the Emergency Management Association of Wyoming and is a licensed amateur radio operator, call sign KE7EKA. He is a member of the Campbell County Volunteer Fire Department, certified as a Firefighter II in the State of Wyoming, a Hazardous Materials Technician and member of the CCVFD's Hazardous Materials Response Team. David is certified as a Fire Instructor 1, a Wyoming Contract Trainer for "Awareness Level" (Hazardous Materials Training) for the State Emergency Response Commission and has instructed for the Wyoming Emergency Management Agency. He has completed the FEMA Terrorism Planner course, has taken specialized training in EMS Decontamination, Explosives for Fire and HazMat Responders at the Idaho Hazardous Materials Training Center in Pocatello, Idaho, completed the EPA Sampling for Hazardous Materials course, is certified as a Dispatch Recorder by the National Wildland Coordination Group, and holds an Engine Operator Card. He is also certified as a Basic Emergency Medical Care - First Responder by the Wyoming Department of Health. David is a member of the Campbell County Local Emergency Planning Committee and has been a member of the Wyoming Association of Broadcasters

Board of Directors, the CamPlex Heritage Center Advisory Board in Gillette and the Campbell County Parks and Recreation Department Board of Directors. Because of his work following the Wright Tornado on August 12th, 2005, David was named Citizen of the Year by the Campbell County Chamber of Commerce. He received the Gordon Kent Emergency Manager of the Year award from the Emergency Management Association of Wyoming in 2002.

Melinda Koenig, Psy.D. is a licensed clinical psychologist and Director of a large outpatient psychiatric clinic of a multi-site hospital in Manhattan. A former head of outpatient mental health services for the US Navy, she has focused on the particular stresses faced by healthcare professionals and hospital staff as they are called to respond to a wide range of emergencies. She is the Chairperson for her Department of Psychiatry's emergency response program and has written the emergency response plan for staff surge requirements in disaster response, which includes an emphasis on training for maximum resilience. As Corporate Coordinator for Mental Health Disaster Preparedness for the six-hospital corporation in New York, including St. Luke's-Roosevelt Hospital, she is responsible for initiating, implementing, and coordinating staff emergency preparedness and support.

Heidi Heft LaPorte Areas of Expertise: Research methods, mental health, consumer satisfaction in health care settings, database applications for social service Degrees: MSW, DSW, Wurzweiler School of Social Work, Yeshiva University Assistant Professor.

Nancy L. Day, CTS, CTM is a Certified Trauma Specialist with the Association of Traumatic Stress Specialists (ATSS), a Certified Traumatologist, and a Certified Advanced Traumatic Incident Reduction (TIR) & Metapsychology facilitator and trainer. TIR is a procedure best known for its use as an effective tool for use in the rapid resolution of trauma-related conditions, including PTSD. Nancy is also a volunteer on a CISM team in Kansas City, specializing in the follow-up stage of crisis response. Never satisfied with mediocre, Nancy focuses on procedures that help individuals get results quickly, privately and without negative side effects.

Stewart Anderson is an Adjunct instructor for State of Wyoming Emergency Management, Wyoming Law Enforcement Academy, Wyoming Fire Academy, Casper Community College, South Dakota Office of Emergency Management. Contract employee for Kenyon International Disaster Services. Certifications in the following areas: WY P.O.S.T. General Instructor, EMT-B., Certified Professional Peace Officer, CERT coordinator for Natrona County, Coordinator – Natrona County Emergency Management.

Index

Printed in the United States
69802LV00001B

9 781932 690378